The Price of Disobedience

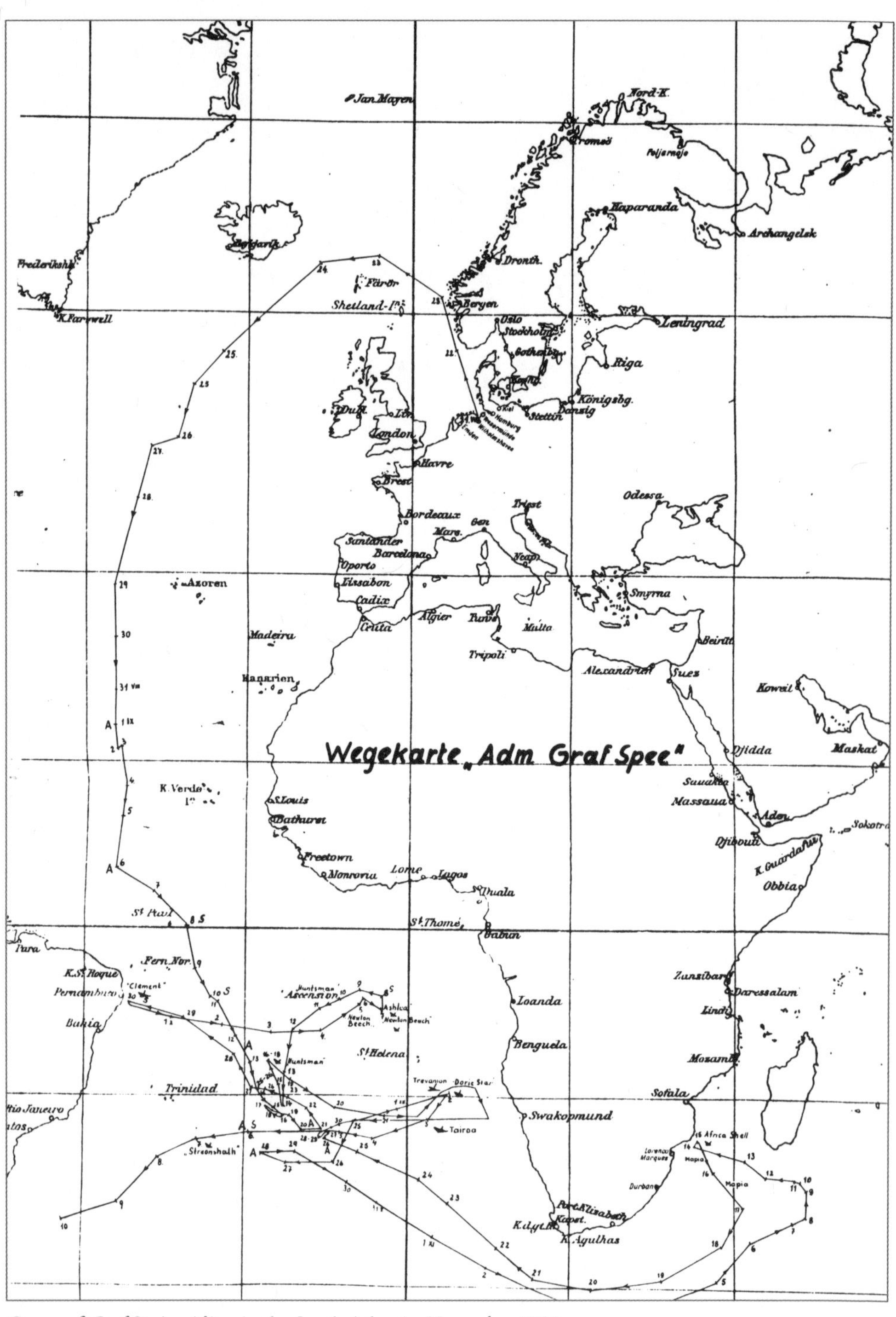

Course of *Graf Spee*'s raiding in the South Atlantic, November 1939.

The Price of Disobedience

The Battle of the River Plate Reconsidered

Eric J. Grove

Naval Institute Press

First published in 2000 by Sutton Publishing Limited, Phoenix Mill, Thrupp, Stroud, Gloucestershire, GL5 2BU

Published and distributed in the United States of America and Canada by the Naval Institute Press, 291 Wood Road, Annapolis, MD 21402-5034

Library of Congress Catalog Card Number: 00-108385

ISBN 1-55750-429-6

To Sylvia
who still cannot quite
see what the fuss was
all about

Manufactured in Great Britain.

Contents

List of Illustrations

(The photograph of Langsdorff appears by kind permission of the Bibliothek für Zeitgeschichte, Stuttgart)

Introduction

When my United Kingdom publisher invited me to do a book on a naval battle I wondered which to choose? Were there new perspectives to be taken on any action? I then thought of the River Plate. Editing and then writing short accounts of the battle had emphasised for me the tragic role of Langsdorff in disobeying orders and seeking action. This shed new light on his decision to shoot himself after the scuttling. It soon became clear that the standard current account, *The Battle of the River Plate* by Dudley Pope (William Kimber, London, 1956), excellent and readable though it still is (it was reissued to mark the sixtieth anniversary in 1999), could be added to in terms of information to which he did not have access when he wrote it in the 1950s. The other major book on the Plate, Eugen Millington-Drake's *The Drama of Graf Spee and the Battle of the Plate*, published in 1964, was not intended to be a connected, analytical account but a 'documentary anthology'. In fact, it is a rich seam of source material that has not been sufficiently mined and it was of considerable use in composing this account.

It has proved remarkably easy to unearth new material on the battle, to make original interpretations; and it is on this contribution to knowledge that the worth, if any, of this volume rests. Many have helped in its production, notably the two sons of Admiral Harwood, Henry and Stephen, distinguished Naval officers in their own right, who have been unstintingly helpful in giving access to their father's papers. Also of great assistance has been Jill Quaife, former secretary to Sir Eugen Millington-Drake. The British Maritime Charitable Foundation also passed on an extremely useful collection of papers and pictures belonging to Robin Lumley. The staffs of the Public Record Office and the Documents Department of the Imperial War Museum are to be thanked for being their usual efficient selves. My PhD student, Dr James Yates, provided vital research assistance and Dr Andrea Elner of the University of Reading gave crucial help with German translation. Great generosity with the provision of materials was also given, and patience shown, by one of the world's greatest experts on the battle, Graham Beeson of Auckland, New Zealand, whom I met on a visit there in 1997 and who has been unstinting in the provision of his extensive collection of material on the action. Elizabeth Grove compiled the index in her usual rapid and efficient fashion.

The closing years of the 1990s have been very difficult ones for a number of personal reasons and many, not least my long-suffering publishers, have had to show remarkable forbearance. I thank all who have given support in this trying time, but especially my dear friend Sylvia Miles, who provided the inspiration to finish the project and to whom the book is therefore dedicated.

Eric Grove
University of Hull
September 2000

Part One
Panzerschiff

CHAPTER ONE

The 'Pocket Battleship'

The Treaty of Versailles of 1919 limited the major units of the postwar Reichsmarine to six pre-Dreadnought battleships as coastal defence 'armoured ships' ('Cuirassés' in the French of the Treaty, 'Panzerschiffe' in German) and six light cruisers. In 1920, the victorious Allies allowed Germany the bonus of two vessels of each class in reserve (although no more than four ships were usually operational at any one time). Replacement was allowed after ships became twenty years old with vessels no larger than 10,000 tons and 6,000 tons respectively. The precise means of determining these displacements was not specified; nor, contrary to popular view, was the maximum calibre of the replacement ships' armament. That question was left as a matter of negotiation between the Germans and the Conference of Allied Ambassadors set up by the Treaty. The ambassadors did allow the armament of the new cruiser *Emden* to be increased to 5.9-in. from the 4.1-in. of the old Gazelle and Bremen class ships with which the Reichsmarine had been left. But the Germans decided not to push their luck; it was felt it would not be worthwhile even to try to get Panzerschiff armament increased beyond the largest guns carried by the pre-Dreadnoughts, i.e. 11-in.[1]

Settling for a limited calibre of main armament also made design sense, as the Reichsmarine struggled in the 1920s to produce a new type of larger, armoured ship. The existing fleet of Panzerschiffe comprised the three Deutschland class pre-Dreadnoughts *Hanover, Schlesien* and *Schleswig Holstein* launched in 1905–6, and all five of the Braunschweig class, *Braunschweig*, *Elsass*, *Hessen*, *Preussen* and *Lothringen*, launched in 1902–04. *Preussen* and *Lothringen* were disarmed as minesweeper tenders and first in line for replacement. They carried mixed-calibre armaments of four 11-in. and fourteen 6.7-in. guns. Speed was 18.5 knots but protection was not very good; one Deutschland class ship, *Pommern*, had blown up after being torpedoed by British destroyers at the Battle of Jutland, the most expensive German loss of the battle in human terms. There was an insuperable problem in balancing the most powerful armament possible with German-style heavy protection and adequate speed, all on a 10,000 ton displacement – even one based on the more liberal Washington Treaty 'standard' formula that allowed a little more margin than that previously used.

The main role considered for new Panzerschiffe in the 1920s was not, as is commonly thought, commerce raiding. It was to engage a French squadron that might be sent into the Baltic in support of Poland, whose territory cut Prussia in two. The French commitment under the Franco-Polish Treaty was a cruiser squadron, but it was thought that France planned to send the modernised semi-Dreadnought *Voltaire* in support of her cruisers. *Voltaire* had a speed of 19 knots and was armed with four 13-in. and twelve 9.4-in. guns that the Germans thought could deliver 6.25 tons of shell per minute at 35 km. range. To deal with this threat, that totally outgunned existing German ships, in 1923 two designs were considered: I/10, a high-speed, 32-knot, enlarged Emden-type cruiser, armed with eight 8.2-in. guns; and a more novel II/10, a steam-powered armoured ship with four 15-in. guns, a speed of 22 knots but thinner armour than the existing pre-Dreadnoughts (200-mm belt against 240-mm on the best of the older ships, and 30-mm deck armour against 35-mm). Neither was considered good enough to go further.

With Germany wracked by the inflation crisis it was perhaps unsurprising that work on the new armoured ships lapsed in 1924, but it began again the following year, enthusiastically backed by Admiral Zenker, the new Chef der Marineleitung appointed at the beginning of October. Zenker had commanded the battlecruiser *Von der Tann* at Jutland. Three new sketch designs were produced, II/30 armed with six 12-in. guns (two forward and four aft) with 200-mm armour, a more lightly armoured (180-mm) IV/30 with the guns all forward to save weight – and to allow, additionally, four 5.9-in. secondary guns – and V/30, with triple 12-in. guns fore and aft and a 180-mm belt. All three designs were diesel engined to save weight.

These sketch designs were discussed at a conference in mid-May 1925, and the consensus was that all three were too lightly protected. First World War German capital ships had carried armoured belts 250–350-mm thick. To allow more displacement for armour, it was suggested that twin 12-in. guns capable of 25 rounds per minute might be able to deliver enough fire, rather than six 11-in. Two designs armed with four 12-in. guns were therefore produced, VI/30 with twin turrets fore and aft, and VII/30 with turrets all forward. Civilian doubts about the acceptability of 12-in. guns also led to 11-in. designs being produced, I/28 with triple turrets fore and aft and II/28 with three twins arranged like II/30.

A meeting held on 27 May 1925 to discuss these designs was inconclusive. Plans for new Panzerschiffe were in any case somewhat academic at this time. Germany's ability to build any heavy guns was limited by the French occupation of the Ruhr; and the restricted design facilities of the Reichsmarine's Construction Office were too preoccupied with the two new Königsberg class cruisers and the '1923' torpedo boat flotilla to begin detailed design work on armoured ships. It was nevertheless hoped to begin Panzerschiff 'A' the following year. Despite its other priorities, the weary Construction Office produced yet more new 11-in. armed designs: I/35, a slow, well-protected, monitor-style ship with a single triple turret forward and twin secondary turrets aft; and a more lightly protected VIII/30 with twins fore and aft and secondary guns amidships and aft.

The French withdrawal from the Ruhr in July 1926 allowed the Reichsmarine to think more seriously about heavily armed ships, while the shipyards were in need of further orders. So, another meeting was held on 13 August to see if one of the available designs offered a good enough basis for a Panzerschiff to be ordered. Neither did, and it was decided to build instead an extra 'K'-class cruiser, *Köln*, and the second '1924' flotilla of new torpedo boats.

All this delay may have been as well, as fleet manœuvres in 1926 led to a major reassessment of the armoured ship concept. High speed, it was now argued, should become a major priority as it offered great tactical advantages. Thus two new designs were drawn up, I/M26 and II/M26. These were 'battleship cruiser'-type ships with an armament of six 11-in. guns and high speed, 28 knots. Armour, however, was only 100-mm thick, the protection of a light cruiser rather than a capital ship.

Zenker was unhappy with these ships and, at a meeting in January 1927, once more called for the design of more heavily protected vessels. A belt comparable to the 250-mm of his old *Von der Tann* was necessary to hold the Baltic entrances against French ships that (it was now assessed) might include the 13.4-in. armed super-Dreadnoughts of the Bretagne class. Wearily, the designers returned to their drawing boards and produced, by March 1927, new designs for 250-mm protected ships with twin turrets forward. These were capable of making only 18 knots, the operational speed generally credited to the French battle squadrons. French Dreadnoughts and super-Dreadnoughts, however, could, at least notionally, make 20 knots and an alternative 24-knot German ship was placed on the table alongside the slow monitors.

At a meeting on 7 March 1927, the advantages of still higher speed were reasserted. An important new formula was proposed. The new Panzerschiffe would require superior speed to escape from anything they could not fight and superior fighting power to deal with anything they could not outrun. The Washington Treaty, to which France was subject, set the standards over which the new ship had to be superior in at least one respect: the British *Nelson* and *Rodney* seemed to demonstrate that a 35,000 ton, 16-in. gun capital ship of balanced design could not make much more than 23–24 knots. Faster cruisers were limited to 10,000 tons and 8-in. guns. Thus, the minimum requirement for the new formula was 11-in. guns and at least 26 knots.

In June 1927, Zenker wrote to the senior admirals of the Reichsmarine. The optimal requirement, he said, was a ship capable of defeating French capital ships *and* supporting light cruisers against 10,000 ton, 8-in. cruisers. The problem was that neither of these criteria could be met on a 10,000 ton displacement. Four options, said Zenker, were on the table:

A 4x15-in. guns, 250-mm armour, 18-knots;
B1 6x12-in. guns, 250-mm armour, 18-knots;
B2 6x12-in. guns, 200-mm armour, 21 knots;
C 6x11-in. guns, 100mm armour, 26–27 knots.

By this time, Zenker considered C, a 'small battle cruiser' as the Naval Command rather optimistically called it, given its protection, the only practical option. Higher speed was absolutely essential to evade battleships and engage cruisers. A minimum of six guns were deemed necessary for fire control reasons and 11-in. guns were the maximum calibre possible to produce a balanced design of such a ship. This meant no politically bruising confrontation with the Allies would be necessary. Two units were to be built in the first instance, Panzerschiffe 'A' and 'B', with the possibility of a larger ship being agreed with the Allies later.

So Design 'C', basically I/M26, was taken as the basis of the new Panzerschiff, as Zenker insisted she still be called publicly, in literal fulfilment of Versailles. Under the leadership of the head of the Reichsmarine's Construction Office, Dr Paul Presse, the hard-pressed draughtsmen drew up a novel design using welding and light metals to minimise displacement. The diesel propulsion of the sketch designs was retained, as the eight double-acting, nine-cylinder 56,000 h.p. MAN engines occupied the minimum length within the ship, thus saving weight. The engines themselves, however, were heavy and offered no intrinsic weight advantage. Indeed, Presse's team had great difficulty in squeezing all the required characteristics onto the 10,000-ton ship and thinner armour had to be resorted to. Main belt armour consisted of two strips, 80-mm above 60-mm, angled outwards to increase protection; there were armoured bulkheads fore and aft, also 60-mm thick. The ship came out 1,700 tons overweight; but she at least looked plausibly like a 10,000-ton ship, and the Versailles restrictions had proved most effective in limiting German design options. In April 1928, the detailed sketch design was approved and the ship was ordered from the Deutsche Werke at Kiel on 17 August 1928. Defence Minister Gröner guided the programme through a difficult Reichstag. The full drawings were ready by 28 December, and the ship was laid down on 9 February 1929.

By this time Zenker had been forced to step down because of political scandal. He was replaced by Admiral Erich Raeder, who would lead the German Navy for the next fourteen years. Raeder, asked by Gröner in 1929 to set out the need for larger warships, argued that war with Britain had to be avoided as her strength and position doomed Germany at sea from the start. France remained the major possible opponent; and Raeder seems to have foreseen the new armoured ships using the long range granted by their diesels to cruise at length in the North Sea, preventing a French blockade of German ports. Their speed would avoid the covering French battlefleet and allow descents on the blockading French cruisers. In no sense were the new ships being designed to prey on the British Empire's seaborne trade.

The new Panzerschiff was not only controversial at home. France and Italy stated that, because of the new German ship, they were not willing to extend the Washington restrictions on their fleets. France planned a direct counter in the shape of a fast, 29.5-knot battleship of 26,500 tons armed with eight 13-in. guns. Britain, hosting a naval conference in London in 1930, called on Germany to delay armoured ship construction until 1937 because of this negative arms control impact. The German Government offered to cancel their new ship in return for Germany's being allowed into the Naval Treaty system on a basis of 25 per cent of British and American strength in capital ships. This was not agreed, and construction of the Panzerschiff went ahead. She was christened *Deutschland* at her launch on 19 May 1931, a name that put her in the same tradition as her pre-Dreadnought predecessors, and was commissioned on 1 April 1933, only weeks after the Nazis had gained power. Panzerschiff 'B', notionally to replace *Lothringen* (already sold for scrap), was not laid down, at the Marinewerft, Wilhelmshaven, until 25 June 1931; the economic depression providing a less-than favourable environment for naval expenditure. Her design was modified with a broader beam, and a large, tower-type foremast was also adopted. Displacement seems not to have been unduly affected because of lighter shafting arrangements, auxiliary machinery, a redesigned armour belt, with a 50-mm upper belt, and 40–50-mm bulkheads. In the new political climate, she was named after Germany's brave and aggressive Hochseeflotte commander of the First World War, Admiral Scheer. She was launched the very day *Deutschland* was commissioned and entered service in November 1934.

The question of a third ship, Panzerschiff 'C', had been a matter of yet more controversy in Germany. The new French ships seemed to undermine the effectiveness of the existing design. On 28 June 1932, Raeder chaired a Ship Replacement conference. The existing pre-Dreadnoughts were on their last legs. Only *Hessen* and the three Deutschlands remained. They were slow, ill-armed and weakly protected, comparing badly even with other pre-Dreadnoughts of their own obsolete generation. They could not support cruisers and were useless for trade defence; they were even inadequate for coastal defence. New major units were essential for naval and political reasons, preferably of a larger, 11-in. type to deal with the new French ships. It was hoped that Versailles might be abandoned, either unilaterally or by agreement; but, if not, a Panzerschiff 'C' should be ordered by October 1932. This would also provide employment for 3,000 men. Her propulsion might be steam, depending on experience with the latest steam plant in the new cruiser *Leipzig* and the diesels in the minelayer *Bremse.* Opinion varied, with the Construction Office coming out in favour of diesels. Eventually diesels were decided on for 'C' because of their greater range potential. The order was placed with the Marinewerft, Wilhelmshaven on 23 August 1932.

'C', officially a replacement for *Braunschweig*, was laid down on Slip II beside 'B', already taking shape on Slip I. Her engines were similar to her sister's, albeit heavier still, and she had some significant improvements. Protection was better, with a belt of increased height and length, 80-mm above 50-mm.[2] At the ends of the belt were 100-mm armoured transverse bulkheads, a major increase over the 40–60-mm bulkheads of the earlier ships. Between the 125-mm thick barbettes were 40-mm vertical bulkheads in front of an armoured deck of varying thickness, ranging from 70-mm above the magazines to 20-mm elsewhere on the centreline; normal thickness of the armoured deck outside the bulkheads was 40-mm out to the inward-inclined 40-mm anti-torpedo bulkheads stretching down to the ship's bottom, and 30-mm beyond to the main belt on the ship's sides. There was a lower armoured deck 45-mm thick protecting the steering gear. This extra protection helped increase displacement in the third Panzerschiff to 12,100 tons standard, 16,200 full load.

****

Panzerschiff 'C' was named *Admiral Graf Spee* when she was launched on 30 June 1934. She was christened by Huberta von Spee, daughter of Vizeadmiral Graf von Spee, hero of the German victory at Coronel off the coast of Chile in 1914, before he went down with his flagship *Scharnhorst* off the Falkland Islands shortly afterwards. The new ship carried a large battle honour plate inscribed 'Coronel' on the forward wall of the tower superstructure. *Graf Spee* was commissioned on 6

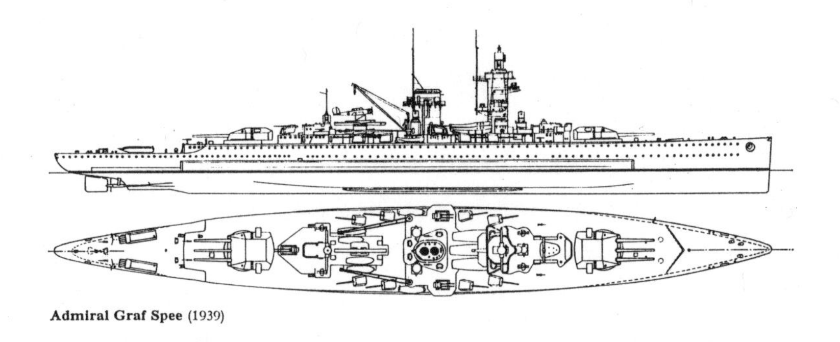

Profile of a Panzerschiff: *Graf Spee* on the drawing board (1939).

January 1936. On her trials, her diesels proved capable of driving her at 28.5 knots at 240 r.p.m. on her twin shafts. This made her, by a narrow margin, the fastest of the 'pocket battleships' – as the Panzerschiffe were soon nicknamed. Her fuel consumption was also better.

Admiral Graf Spee was not a particularly large ship. At just over 610-feet long overall she was shorter than contemporary large cruisers of more conventional design such as the British Counties or the French Duquesnes or Suffrens. She was, however, somewhat broader in the beam at almost 71-feet. This was a reflection of her exceptionally powerful armament for a ship of her size, comprising a triple 11-in. turret fore and aft. The turrets were armoured to 140-mm on their faces and the 54.5 calibre SKC/28 guns, of a new design specially created for the ships, could elevate to 40 degrees, giving a maximum range of 36,475 metres. The guns had to return to 2 degrees elevation for loading, which slowed down the rate of fire. If all went well, each turret could fire its three guns every 20–25 seconds. Two charges were used with each round, a main 156.5-lb. charge with a brass case and a 79.4-lb. fore charge. Three types of shell were available, armour-piercing, base-fused high-effect and nose-fused high-effect. The H.E. shells weighed just under 700-lbs and the A.P.s just over 725-lbs. To maintain the *Graf Spee* tradition, each turret was christened after one of the First World War admiral's cruisers, *Scharnhorst* and *Gneisenau*.[3]

The secondary armament consisted of eight single 5.9-in. S.K.C./28 guns in single M.P.L.C./28 shield mountings, four on each beam. The guns could elevate to 35 degrees and had a range at this elevation of 22,000 metres. A single cartridge case was used to fire 100-lb H.E. shells (both base- and nose-fused) and illumination rounds. Anti-aircraft protection in *Graf Spee* comprised three twin 3.5-in. gun mounts, one aft and one on each beam, with a light armament of four twin 37-mm and eight 20-mm weapons. This was a relatively heavy A.A. suite for its time.

Main armament fire control was provided from three control positions, as was the German practice. One was on top of the tower foremast, one in the heavily armoured conning tower abaft the bridge and one aft, abaft the seaplane catapult. The foremast and after control positions had 10-metre baselength stereoscopic range finders, the conning tower a six-metre rangefinder. Both the conning tower and the foremast position had two directors and the after position one. These positions fed range and bearing data to the main transmitting station below the conning tower where it was converted by mechanical analogue computers into a fire control solution for transmission to the guns; there was a back-up main armament T/S below the after 4.1-in. mount. The main control positions also fed the secondary armament T/S. Doctrine for the use of the armament was that both main armament turrets should engage a single target, firing single turret three gun salvos every ten or twelve seconds to obtain the range as quickly as possible.[4] While this was going on, the secondary armament could engage a different target if desired. There was a high-angle director either side of the funnel. Aft on the quarterdeck were two quadruple 21-in. torpedo mountings protected by armoured shields. There were six powerful 150-cm searchlights, two on each side of the foremast and four on a platform around the funnel.[5]

All this made *Graf Spee* a formidable foe for a single enemy cruiser that chose to stand and fight – but any number of enemies would be a serious problem, as she could not divide the fire of her main armament. Moreover, any ship built down to such a limited, fixed displacement was bound to have serious weaknesses. One fundamental flaw was weak armour. 'Pocket battleship' was an inaccurate and misleading nickname, as it implied battleship standards of protection, a reputation it was in the interest of friend and foe alike to foster. Even 'Panzerschiff' was misleading: in fact, in First World War terms, the *Graf Spee* was fundamentally a 'light cruiser'. Only her turrets and barbettes were armoured above contemporary cruiser standards and even then not up to the standards of contemporary battleships: *Dunkerque*'s turrets were over twice as thickly armoured. The closest previous ships in concept were the somewhat bigger British 15-in. armed 'large light cruisers', *Glorious* and *Courageous*; much-maligned brainchildren of Fisher, which had been converted into aircraft carriers after the war. Interestingly, these lightly protected but fast vessels had also been built with Baltic scenarios in mind. Armoured cruisers of the 1914 'pre-Dreadnought' generation, such as Admiral Graf Spee's *Scharnhorst* and *Gneisenau*, had belts about twice as thick as *Graf Spee*'s – as did the earlier British battlecruisers. Later British battlecruisers had belts three times as thick! Contemporary British 6-in. armed cruisers of the 1930s had armoured belts of at least the same thickness as *Graf Spee*'s, increasing to 114-mm in *Belfast* and *Edinburgh*. The contemporary French 8-in. armed *Algerie* had a 120mm belt. *Graf Spee* was an averagely protected and very heavily armed cruiser, not a capital ship.[6]

Any ship with large guns that a Panzerschiff chose to fight would make short work of her; a proper battlecruiser like the British *Hood*, *Repulse* or *Renown*, or one of the new French fast battleships, would be a fatal threat. The armour system was supposed to keep out 8-in. shells while the German armoured ship demolished her weaker opponent, but it was marginal even for that. Moreover, the secondary armament with its semi-open shields would be vulnerable to shells that did not penetrate the ship herself.

There were other problems too. The diesel propulsion system, while giving major advantages in responsiveness and fuel economy – and, therefore, range (*Graf Spee* could cruise over 16,000 miles at 18 knots) – was subject to serious reliability and vibration problems. Moreover, the whole design of the ship was fundamentally overloaded and seakeeping suffered, the straight stem and low forecastle being particular weaknesses. The lower control positions forward were often made useless because of spray, forcing the captain to con and fight the ship from an unprotected position at the top of the tower foremast. The latter was too prominent and provided an excellent aiming point for an enemy.

Tank trials were carried out in 1938 and showed that the hull lines of the Panzerschiff were very poor. Lengthening and broadening with a new design of bow were required to improve stability and seaworthiness. Rebuilding was considered, which would solve other problems also; for example, the vulnerable secondary armament was to get extra protection. The work was to take place between January 1941 and December 1943, *Graf Spee* being the second ship to be modified. Events overtook these plans. *Graf Spee* received only limited modifications on refit in 1938. Her A.A. armament was further strengthened with 4.1-in. guns replacing the 3.5s and four extra ¾-in. being added. The foremast searchlights were also removed and replaced by a single light mounted on the forward part of the tower.[7]

This seems to have been connected with the fitting of an experimental 'Seetakt' radar, a 60-cm wavelength FuMG38G set, the first naval radar in the world. This was intended primarily for rangefinding purposes; but it did not have sufficient bearing accuracy and was used for surveillance instead. The effective range of the radar was increased from about 5–8 kilometres to 15 as experience with the set grew, still far less than the range of the ship's superb optical equipment; the stereoscopic rangefinder on the foremast could pick out targets at over 50 km.[8] The radar was therefore most useful at night and in poor visibility. To house the set, a new cylindrical structure with a mounting for a mattress antenna was added to the foremast director control tower. The antenna could be removed or covered for security. This secrecy seems to have worked and the British seem to have had no inkling of *Graf Spee*'s radar capability. Her position as the most electronically advanced unit in the Kriegsmarine was confirmed by the ship being also fitted with what would now be called E.S.M. gear, a radio monitoring unit listening out for interesting electronic emissions.[9]

Graf Spee was first commissioned, by Kapitän Konrad Patzig, on 6 January 1936. She joined the fleet after trials on 9 May and became fleet flagship just in time for the review held at the end of the month in Kiel Bay to mark the dedication of the naval memorial there. In June she made her first test foray into the Atlantic, visiting the Canary Islands. *Graf Spee* was soon to see more serious duty in Spanish waters with the outbreak of the Civil War in July occasioning German naval patrols to look after Germany's interests and to cover ships carrying supplies for Franco's forces. Her first tour of duty was from 20 August to 9 October and she returned in December flying the flag of Rear Admiral von Fischel, Flag Officer Reconnaissance Forces. This deployment lasted until February 1937, and a third round of duty followed from 2 March. The last week of this deployment in May was marked by rather different work as a much-photographed participant in the 1937 Coronation review. Another two-week tour off Spain followed in June–July, after which *Graf Spee* returned to the Baltic for fleet exercises in September and a visit to Sweden.

At the beginning of October 1937, Patzig handed over command to Kapitän Walter Warzecha. He took the ship on a visit to Norway at the end of the year and on the last of her five Spanish deployments, in February 1938. Unlike her sisters, *Graf Spee* had a relatively quiet time off Spain, neither being attacked, like *Deutschland*, or engaging in retaliatory bombardments, like *Scheer*. The Summer of 1938 saw another visit to Norwegian waters on a training cruise and a review at

Kiel in honour of Admiral Horthy, the distinguished Austro-Hungarian Naval officer who had become Hungarian dictator. Warzecha had only a year in command of *Graf Spee* before being replaced by Hans Langsdorff on 1 October 1938, just after the Munich agreements had delayed for a year the onset of war. Langsdorff's first voyages with the ship were Atlantic training cruises in October and November, with visits to Vigo, Tangier, Bilbao and Portuguese ports.

More operational duty followed in March 1939, when all three Panzerschiffe covered the occupation of the Baltic port of Memel. The following month the German Navy began a major fleet deployment to carry out exercises and show the flag in the Atlantic. *Graf Spee*, flying the flag of Admiral Böhm, provided the core of this group, with three light cruisers, seven destroyers, a submarine tender and three U-boat flotillas. Exercises were carried out and visits made to Spanish ports and Lisbon. *Deutschland* joined the squadron before it returned to Germany on 16 May. The Spanish Civil War was now over and *Graf Spee* formed part of the escort for the German Condor Legion on its return home at the end of May.

By August 1939, with the Polish crisis threatening to bring about Raeder's previous nightmare of war with Britain, *Graf Spee* and *Deutschland* were Germany's only two available major surface units. *Scheer* was suffering an acute bout of 'dieselitis' and was capable only of static anti-aircraft duties at Wilhelmshaven; while the larger battleships *Scharnhorst* and *Gneisenau*, built as answers to the Dunkerques after the Anglo-German naval agreement had legalised Germany's denunciation of Versailles, were not properly worked-up after refits to improve their seaworthiness. The new heavy cruiser *Admiral Hipper* was running trials after similar work. It would be the two 'pocket battleships' that were to start the surface war at sea.

CHAPTER TWO

The Raider

In the Spring of 1938, Germany began to revise its naval thinking as it had become only too clear that the British as well as the French opposed Germany's eastern expansion. Hitler issued an official directive that Britain should now be considered a potential enemy. Raeder went along with this transformation of policy – on the assumption that the Kriegsmarine would be given a period of years to complete a naval build-up. In a study completed in the Summer of 1938, the German Navy decided that even then the only option was a cruiser *guerre de course* against merchant shipping in the Atlantic carried out both by major surface units – including larger, faster pocket battleships – and U-boats. Hitler wanted more and tried to embark on a major battlefleet build up in early 1939, but the Polish crisis forced an emergency return to a *guerre de course* with available assets, inadequate though they were. It was a sign of the confusion in German strategy at this time that, as late as 22 August 1939, the Führer was assuring Raeder, who had already sent his ships to sea, and the other heads of his fighting services that war with Britain and France need not necessarily be expected. A final settlement of the Polish question might be postponed to avoid such a conflict. Just over a week later, Germany would be at war.[1]

Admiral Raeder was an expert on commerce raiding operations, having written the official history of surface raiders after the First

World War. One of his prime conclusions was that their operations would have been much more effective if the German cruiser commanders had avoided action with Allied ships. Officers such as Graf von Spee himself had let their aggressive instincts run away with them and sought engagements. This could have only one eventual result, given the Allies' dominant sea power. Raeder was determined that his raiders would not make the same mistake, especially as the German Navy was in an even weaker position in 1939 than it had been in 1914.[2]

Despite Hitler's confidence that the Polish crisis would not lead to war, Raeder began to make precautionary moves at the end of July. On the 27th, orders were issued to load the naval auxiliary tanker *Altmark* with stores for the *Graf Spee* that had been designated for raiding operations in the South Atlantic. *Altmark* sailed from Wilhelmshaven on 2 August for Port Arthur, Texas, where she picked up 9,400 tons of diesel fuel. On 17 August *Graf Spee* was recalled from torpedo firings to be docked, overhauled and stored. After frenzied activity she sailed from Wilhelmshaven on 21 August. She was carrying a complement of 1,134 officers and men, including cypher experts from the *B-Dienst* to exploit her E.S.M. gear and five reservists from the mercantile marine who knew the trade routes and movements well, and who would act as prize captains. The Panzerschiff carefully timed her passage off the Norwegian coast, through the Iceland–Faeroes gap and across the busiest Atlantic shipping areas, taking advantage of darkness for concealment. The ship's E.S.M., radar and excellent optical equipment were also used to avoid any close encounter that might lead to the ship being reported.[3]

This game of cat-and-mouse greatly appealed to Hans Langsdorff, *Graf Spee*'s commanding officer of almost a year. He had been born on 20 March 1894, in Bergen auf Rugen, four years before Germany set itself the task of becoming a major naval power. The young Langsdorff wished to associate himself with this enterprise; and, on 1 April 1912, became an officer cadet. He soon made his mark, passing out top of his class. He specialised in the technically demanding field of torpedo work and, during the First World War, was torpedo officer – first in the cruiser *Medusa*, and then the battleship *Grosser Kurfurst*, in which Langsdorff served at Jutland. In late 1916 he was given his first command, that of a drifter operating in support of the High Sea Fleet U-boats. His task was to meet incoming U-boats and lead them through the minefields. He had been ordered to show no lights, which meant he had great difficulty in finding his charges. His second-in-command, an old warrant officer, gave Langsdorff some advice. The drifter's orders only stated it should show no *white* lights; other colours were possible, the older man said, winking. So a blue light was rigged and the problem of finding the U-boats disappeared. Langsdorff had learned an important lesson about superior orders: they had not always to be obeyed to the letter, if higher objectives had greater priority to the man on the spot.

Langsdorff rose to command a minesweeping flotilla, was awarded the Iron Cross and by the end of the war had become recognised as one of the best officers in the German Navy. He was an obvious choice for selection as one of the elite of the old Imperial Navy that would command the Weimar Republic's Reichsmarine. Langsdorff's social skills – he had courtesy and charm and a well-developed sense of humour – also made him an excellent candidate for service at the highest political levels. As a thirty year-old Korvettenkapitän (Commander) he was appointed liaison officer between the Reichswehr and the Reichsmarine. He became Aide-de-Camp to General Schleicher, the Minister of Defence and then Chief-of-Staff to the Commander-in-Chief of the Navy. Despite the murder of his former chief, like many naval officers, Langsdorff seems to have welcomed Hitler's coming to power. The British captains who spoke to him in *Graf Spee* found him to be a man of high ideals and, like virtually all German naval officers of his generation, a convinced Nazi, though 'not rabidly so'.[4] He took the 'Socialism' in 'National Socialism' seriously, and the British prisoners were intrigued at the 'very socialistic way' in which *Graf Spee* was run. The officers and men ate the same food and discipline was assessed as lax by British standards.[5] Although Langsdorff was seriously disillusioned by the Molotov-Ribbentrop pact of August 1939, and was not so virulently Nazi as his junior officers, he was far from the anti-Nazi conservative – or even liberal – that he has often been portrayed as being. Such a vision was a figment of Allied propaganda.

Graf Spee had already played a role in creating something of a Langsdorff legend within the German navy. When *Graf Spee*, as fleet flagship, had been dispatched to Spanish waters in 1936, Langsdorff had been commanding the accompanying torpedo boat flotilla. As the squadron exercised in the rough waters of the Bay of Biscay, the flagship gave the order to reduce speed to nine knots so the admiral could take lunch in comfort. The 1,000-ton torpedo boats wallowed most uncomfortably in these conditions and eating was impossible. The torpedo boat captains semaphored to Langsdorff their feelings, whereupon the flotilla commander had the temerity to signal the flagship to request to increase speed so they could have lunch too! The fact that the admiral complied with this request clearly demonstrates Langsdorff's fine sense of where and when not to be overawed by authority.

Graf Spee was therefore commanded by one of the best and most highly thought-of officers in the Kriegsmarine. As Admiral Theodor Kranke later remembered of Langsdorff: 'His intellectual powers far above the average, his calm and well-balanced personality, together with his keen sense of humour and his tactical and strategic training were such that we at home, especially his fellow officers of the same year who knew him thoroughly well, had the certainty that he would master the hard task set him.'[6]

The armoured ships – *Deutschland* sailed from Wilhelmshaven with her auxiliary *Westerwald* on 28 August – had orders to be in position for operations in the Atlantic by the beginning of September. Their general conduct was governed by the latest (July 1939) edition of the German battle instructions. These made it clear that Germany's war aims might be limited or more total, as decided by the political leadership of the Reich. On the high seas the task of naval warfare was to attack merchant shipping. 'Combat action, even against inferior naval forces', the Instructions stressed, was 'not an aim in itself and is therefore not to be sought'. The main targets for Atlantic operations would be British and French commercial shipping, and the latter's troopships. Raiders would rely on prizes and neutrals for supplies, within the limitations of international law. Prize regulations were to be strictly observed, with ships being stopped and searched and the safety of the crew ensured, even when a ship was sunk. The use of neutral territory or waters was forbidden but neutral flags could be used as *ruses de guerre* until fire was opened, when the German ensign had to be unfurled.

The Instructions stressed the importance of: 'surprise appearances, followed by immediate withdrawal into the ocean wastes and constant shifting of areas of activity' as the prerequisites of successful action for surface forces. The preferred operational waters were those least likely to contain enemy warships: the South Atlantic, the Indian Ocean and the Pacific. Junctions of merchant traffic were to be avoided. Commanders in war were allowed the right to independent action: 'as expedient to the operational instructions and the commander's own judgment'. No blame would fall on commanders whose ships were sunk in combat or run until their 'operational possibilities were exhausted' and then laid up in safe neutral ports, with the important proviso that, given Britain's influence over neutrals, measures had to be taken: 'without fail, to ensure that on no account the ship falls into enemy hands'. In any case, putting into a neutral port would inform the enemy of one's position. For all his caveats, however, Raeder stressed that he expected aggressiveness from his officers. 'I shall act without mercy,' he wrote in the Instructions, 'against any commander who compromises the honour of the Flag and is found lacking in that energy which alone can bring success and achieve a position of respect for the German Navy. Rather death with honour than strike the flag!'[7]

The Panzerschiffe's more specific orders were issued on 2 August. These stated that if war broke out with Poland, Britain and France would probably intervene as the guarantor powers. Support for commerce raiding was likely only from Spain and Japan and the neutrality of all neutrals was to be respected. If war did break out, enemy merchant shipping was to be disrupted and destroyed by all possible means with the proviso that, in the beginning, operations were to be carried out strictly in accordance with prize law. If unrestricted submarine warfare was declared, Panzerschiffe were to keep out of such zones to avoid attacks caused by mistaken identity, unless special operational zones were designated. An important sentence came next, one that reiterated the fleet's standing orders: '*Enemy naval forces, even if inferior, are only to be engaged if it should further the principal task*' (i.e. war on merchant shipping).

The instructions went on to advise that: 'frequent changes in position in the operational areas will create uncertainty and will restrict enemy merchant shipping even without tangible results. A temporary departure into distant areas will also add to the uncertainty of the enemy'.[8] Langsdorff would act on these instructions to good effect. Such restriction and disruption were as important as destruction in impairing the enemy supply situation. The Germans also calculated, correctly, that the British would not introduce a complete convoy system and that independent shipping – the easiest targets – could be expected.

Graf Spee was allocated a primary operational area on the South America-Cape Verdes-Biscay trade route with, as a secondary area, the South and Central Atlantic sea area, the Cape Town-Cape Verdes route and the Southern Indian Ocean. Langsdorff, however, was authorised to choose *Graf Spee*'s area of operation according to opposition encountered and actual traffic density. Until hostilities commenced he was to wait in an area north-westward of the Cape Verdes between 15° and 25° N and 25° to 40° W, maintaining complete radio silence.

On 31 August, the German armoured pair were informed that German troops were to cross the Polish frontier the next day and that the attitude of Britain and France was uncertain. Langsdorff read the message to *Graf Spee*'s ship's company on the quarterdeck. They were to fire only if fired upon, he announced. By the day of the invasion both ships were in their waiting areas, *Deutschland* south of Greenland and *Graf Spee*, rendezvoused with *Altmark*, south west of the Canaries at 24°20' N, 36°15' W. As the Germans congratulated themselves on their navigational skills, *Graf Spee* filled her bunkers from *Altmark* and transferred across any equipment that Langsdorff regarded as superfluous, such as *Graf Spee*'s heavier ships' boats, the canvas landing mat for the seaplane, and flammable materials. He also gave the auxiliary two of his 20-mm guns so she could defend herself. Refuelling of Panzershiffe was carried out from the stern of the tanker to the bows, rather than by the alongside method later pioneered by the Americans. Replenishment of solids was carried out by boat.

The pair then sailed southward in company. *Graf Spee*'s officers and men had mixed feelings, the officers trying to overcome depression among the sailors by organising sing-songs. A sunny morning on 2 September raised morale. At the daily officers' meeting Langsdorff forbade the officers to listen to the German services of the BBC, and gave them the unwelcome news that Italy was likely to renege on its alliance with Germany and remain neutral. On the fateful Sunday, 3 September, *Graf Spee* picked up the British war telegram broadcast from Rugby ordering the fleet to commence hostilities against Germany. Three quarters of an hour later the German order to commence hostilities against the British arrived, and *Graf Spee* and *Altmark* set out for their first designated operational area, 400–500 miles west of Freetown.

Late on the Sunday Langsdorff received a most unwelcome signal. This informed him of France's declaration of war; however, he was not allowed to engage French shipping. Hitler seems to have felt that a finely tuned policy of pressure against Britain while withholding action against France might split or even neutralise completely the Allied effort in support of the Poles. Langsdorff worried that these instructions made him vulnerable to being reported by a French merchantman, which – unlike a neutral, so violating its neutrality – he would not be allowed to attack. To this consideration was added information from his own intercept staff that Allied shipping had reduced considerably; that convoys, some covered by heavy units, were indeed running and that the seaplane carrier *Albatross* was on its way to Freetown. Langsdorff's feelings of disillusionment and frustration must have been considerable. His Nazi loyalty had been shaken by the Molotov–Ribbentrop pact: now he was being given impossible orders. His decision was therefore to await clarification of his situation before holding up any shipping and to proceed slowly southwards to his primary operational area.

Then, on 5 September, Langsdorff received even more frustrating instructions, prompted in part by the sinking of the *Athenia* on the first day of the war by a U-boat that had mistaken the liner for an armed merchant cruiser. No action was to be taken against passenger ships, even in convoy, because of French and British inactivity. Panzerschiffe raiding was 'inadvisable at present'. Because of suspension of normal merchant shipping and organised search operations against raiders, there was 'a reduced possibility of success' for the German ships. Trade warfare was therefore to be discontinued, and Panzerschiffe were ordered to move, in strict radio silence, away from their operational areas to the Arctic, South Atlantic or Indian Ocean.[9]

Interestingly, these restrictions reflected the views of Raeder as much as Hitler. On 7 September, a conference was held with the Führer to discuss the situation, as the Navy saw it, created by the 'political and military restraint shown by France and the still-hesitant conduct of British warfare'. This meant it was advisable for the Panzerschiffe to withdraw from their operational areas. British trade was apparently being stopped and the Royal Navy directed against German raiders. The risk, it was felt, was out of proportion with the chances of success. Raeder recorded his own views: as Britain could not draw France into the war unconditionally, while France could not see any war aim and was trying to stay out of the war, it was 'possible', after the fall of Poland, that 'France and, perhaps, Great Britain might be ready to accept to a certain extent the situation which has been created in the East. Therefore', he went on, 'an attack should not be forced and our strength should be saved for the time being.' Hitler agreed, and it was confirmed that *Graf Spee* and *Deutschland* were to 'hold back and withdraw for the present'.[10]

Langsdorff had decided to move to the South Atlantic, to a position bounded by the points 11° S, 2° W; 20° S, 25° W; 26° S, 7° W. This triangle lay between the major trade routes Plate–Cape of Good Hope; Plate–UK; Cape–UK. It was unfrequented by merchant shipping or warships and had good weather, suitable for *Graf Spee* and *Altmark* to carry out fuelling, storing and engine overhauls. The two ships arrived in the triangle on 10 September and slowed down so that they could just still steer. *Graf Spee* carried one of the latest Arado 196 seaplanes, which was still suffering from teething troubles. The aircraft was much faster than the Heinkel biplane previously carried, but the speed of alighting on the water caused the engine to be soaked, with deleterious effects on its reliability. The aircraft was, however, serviceable on the morning of 11 September and flew a dawn patrol. Some 29 miles from their ship the German aircrew spotted what it thought were two ships on the distant horizon, one of which seemed to be a British cruiser altering course towards where *Graf Spee* and *Altmark* were preparing to carry out a replenishment. Deciding not to break radio silence, and hoping they had not been spotted, the Arado sped back to the ships and gave a visual warning. Rapidly, Langsdorff recalled his boats and the two ships moved apart and away as rapidly as they could.

The cruiser was HMS *Cumberland*, whom we shall meet again later in this story. She was on passage from Plymouth, having been detached from the Home Fleet to reinforce the cruiser hunting group under Commodore Harwood off Rio. She was zigzagging, hence the alteration of course. If *Cumberland*'s track had been ten miles different she would have spotted the German ships. The resulting action would have been an interesting experiment: a Washington cruiser versus a pocket battleship. It is far from certain that *Graf Spee* would have been victorious. Much would have depended on the initial accuracy of the two sides' guns and the circumstances in which the action began. If the Germans had been caught replenishing, things might well have been serious for them. Between mutually alerted foes the odds would have been with the Germans, nevertheless *Graf Spee* might have suffered significant damage, making her easy meat for the concentration of forces the Allies would certainly have arrayed against her. It had been a lucky escape for Langsdorff, and perhaps also for *Cumberland*. The former studied anxiously his vital radio intercepts to check on whether he had indeed been discovered.

****

It took the Germans most of the rest of the month to decide to escalate the war against Britain. As the Allies showed no sign of making peace, the Navy began to ask for more aggressive measures to be taken against them. On 23 September a meeting was held at Zoppot between the Naval Staff, Hitler and General Keitel, the head of the armed forces command (O.K.W.). It was decided that time to commit the Panzerschiffe was running out, otherwise both their supplies and morale would run low. Hitler agreed they should be committed by the beginning of October as part of an intensification of the Navy's special duty to disrupt British sea transport traffic. He still hoped to drive a wedge between Britain and France, however, and not all restrictions on measures against France were lifted.[11]

Three days later, on the 26th, orders were finally issued to the Panzerschiffe that they were to begin operations against British shipping, using all means within the prize rules to disrupt and destroy it. French ships were, however, still not to be attacked. Langsdorff was also reminded of the Pan-American neutrality zone declared by President Roosevelt, extending out into the Atlantic for up to 600 miles. Operations in the zone were not forbidden, but incidents that might inflame U.S. opinion were to be avoided. Langsdorff was apprised of the latest information on enemy dispositions. The cruisers *Exeter*, *Cumberland*, *Ajax*, *Achilles* and *Dispatch*, the destroyers *Hotspur* and *Havoc* and the submarine *Severn* were reported as being off the east coast of South America. The cruisers *Neptune*, *Danae* and *Capetown*, the submarine *Clyde* and two smaller ships were off the West African coast. Ominously, heavy British units had not been located and it was considered possible that they were being used to cover convoys.

Langsdorff used long reflections in his war diary to help him in his decision making. These give valuable insights into his frame of mind at this stage. He decided that the South American trade route was more valuable to the Allies than the Cape, as Italy's failure to enter the war made use of the Mediterranean still possible. He decided therefore to proceed first off Pernambuco, and sweep southwards to find British ships near the Brazilian coast, which he would attack 'energetically, at the first favourable opportunity'.[12] Then he would withdraw before forces could be collected against him, proceeding between Ascension and St Helena to raid the Cape route. *Altmark* was to remain in the waiting area.

As he moved north-westwards, another signal was received from Admiral Raeder. This reiterated his order that the ship was not to be fully committed against enemy warships. Britain was in need of successes and any gain in British prestige was, therefore, 'undesirable'. On the other hand, the signal went on, 'attacks on shipping by the Panzerschiffe are to be carried on to the fullest extent'.[13] Restrictions on operations by specified areas were, therefore, cancelled. Langsdorff was also told that, as yet, he had little to fear from battlecruisers or carriers in the South Atlantic. He reacted to this signal by deciding to go for shipping in areas previously considered safe. It was necessary to avoid action with *Exeter* or *Cumberland* as a lucky hit might put paid to *Graf Spee*'s raiding career, even if the British ship came off worse in the encounter. His task, he concluded, was to continue raiding for as long as possible, to tie down as many enemy forces as possible.

The length of time he might remain on station was, however, a moot point, as had been touched on in Raeder's meeting with Hitler. When he was ordered back into action, Langsdorff had been at sea for over a month. *Graf Spee*'s diesel engines were clocking up so many hours that they would soon require dockyard overhaul. It was far from certain that *Graf Spee*'s engineers could keep them running themselves. The tropical latitudes in which the ship found herself also required the refrigeration plant to keep the ammunition cool. This required both carbonic acid and arctic oil, both of which were in short supply. Defects in the system also prevented operating north of 5° S.

Posing as *Admiral Scheer*, *Graf Spee* got her first 'trade' at about noon on 30 September. It came in the form of the 5,051-ton Booth Line tramp, *Clement*. Langsdorff approached her head-on to prevent identification and, anxious she might get away, ordered the Arado to bring her to a standstill with machine-gun fire. The seaplane continued her attacks even after Clement hove-to; but this did not prevent Captain Harris and his crew carrying out Admiralty orders to send out the required warning radio message, destroy important papers and damage the engines so the ship could not be taken as a prize by the Germans, who boarded her at 1250 hrs. As the Clement's crew finally took to the boats, *Graf Spee* was about 1,000 yards on her port beam, training her guns on the doomed ship. Captain Harris and his Chief Engineer were taken on board one of *Graf Spee*'s boats and transferred to the Panzerschiff, where they were met by Langsdorff, who apologised courteously for the necessity to sink the ship. Perhaps significantly, *Graf Spee* had difficulty in inflicting the coup de grace, despite the fact that both ships were stopped. Two torpedoes were tried but one missed ahead and the other astern. Then *Graf Spee* tried gunfire; but the poor seakeeping of the ship, even stopped in an Atlantic swell, made accurate shooting a problem The British officers were unimpressed by the number of rounds it took to sink their ship. Attempts to hole her at the waterline took no less than twenty-five 5.9-in. shells before the heavy armament was resorted to. Five 11-in. rounds finally had the ship slipping perpendicularly beneath the waves at 1430 hrs. Now, the Germans began to worry about ammunition expenditure.

Langsdorff contacted the radio station at Pernambuco to alert them of the presence of the boats, signing the message '*Admiral Scheer*'. The Germans also told the merchant seamen which way to take the boats.

The two officers were later transferred to a passing Greek ship, which promised not to contact the British until he made landfall. Langsdorff wanted the presence of '*Scheer*' to be known, to create maximum disruption and confusion. He now made off to the east at 18 knots to see if he could find anything on the Cape route. Reflecting on the damage *Clement*'s crew had done before capture, and hoping to take his next victim by surprise, Langsdorff began to disguise his ship. The prominent tower foremast was painted to look more like a tripod. The disguise worked. Early on the morning of 5 October, a grey-painted tramp hove into *Graf Spee*'s view. Langsdorff kept his ship bows-on and Captain Robinson, of the 4,651 ton *Newton Beech*, on his way with a cargo of maize to join a convoy at Freetown, mistook *Graf Spee* for a French vessel. Only too late did he realise his mistake. A short, weak distress signal was sent before the boarding party arrived, and the Germans were able to capture the secret documents issued to merchant captains,

Newton Beech's signal had been received by another merchantman, who passed it to HMS *Cumberland*. Very unfortunately it was an S.O.S., not a proper R.R.R. signal and so neither ship gave it the proper priority. *Cumberland* maintained wireless silence and *Graf Spee*'s presence went unreported. The Germans' luck held on 9 October when aircraft from the carrier *Ark Royal* spotted *Altmark* disguised as the American *Delmar*. *Ark Royal* sent out another aircraft to investigate further but it failed to find the tanker in the gathering gloom and the carrier moved on.

Two days before her tanker's lucky escape, *Graf Spee* found another victim. She was the 4,200-ton *Ashlea*, carrying 7,300 tons of sugar from the Cape to UK. Captain Pottinger was taken by surprise by the armoured ship's disguise and only realised his mistake when the mysterious warship ordered his vessel to stop, and lowered a boat. He did not have time to make an R.R.R., but delayed the Germans' boarding until he had destroyed confidential papers. Nevertheless, the Germans were able to obtain some useful intelligence from the ship's logbook, as well as seizing sugar and potatoes. *Ashlea*'s crew was transferred to the *Newton Beech* and the former sunk with bombs placed on board. The following day, Langsdorff decided to sink his other prize, as poor-quality coal was compounding the problem of her already low speed. After taking the prisoners on board *Graf Spee*, *Newton Beech* was sunk by scuttling.

The constant drenching in the sea on alighting had caused terminal cracks in the cylinders of the Arado's BMW engine, and it had to be changed for the spare. This lowered Langsdorff's search horizon. Nevertheless, another ship came to *Graf Spee* on 10 October, the 8,300-ton Harrison cargo liner *Huntsman*, on passage from Calcutta to London. She had already reached Suez when she was ordered round the Cape – a serious error by Naval Control of Shipping. Her cargo was a large one, 10,000 tons of tea, carpets, minerals and gum. Commanded by Captain A.H. Brown, a Merseyside-based officer on his last voyage before retirement, *Huntsman*'s crew was composed of fifteen other Europeans and 67 Lascars. *Graf Spee* was flying the French flag, which put Brown at ease. He was soon horrified, however, to see the tricolour lowered and the Reichskriegsflagge raised. *Huntsman* began to send a raider signal, but *Graf Spee* threatened to open fire if this continued and McCorry, the radio officer, was ordered to stop sending. A boarding party was sent across and Brown, perhaps preoccupied by panic among his crew, was unable to burn his secret documents, which fell into German hands. These gave details of British anti-raider precautions which Langsdorff signalled to Berlin, along with details of his successes to date, under the mistaken impression that *Huntsman*'s brief signal must have been received and therefore radio silence was no longer necessary. In the event, neither signal seems to have been picked up by the British. British wireless vigilance was poor at this early stage of the war and not even a false signal sent by Langsdorff on *Huntsman*'s radio to confuse the Allies that she had been attacked by a submarine was detected. *Graf Spee*'s E.S.M. operators were more sharp-eared, and were able to pick up details of the movement of British warships. Their knowledge of Allied codes was also improved by captured documents, a good haul of which were obtained from *Huntsman.* From these papers, Langsdorff learned that the Allies were not scattering their strength over the ocean but concentrating assets at focal points. Shipping not in convoy was being spread out, making it more difficult for raiders to find quarry. In his signal home, Langsdorff asked for the restrictions on his risking full commitment of his ship to be lifted so that he could raise the stakes, ensuring further successes. The germ of an idea was forming in his mind. On 11 October he also learned that *Ajax* had refuelled at Rio the day before.

The cargo liner's large crew precluded it being taken off without affecting *Graf Spee*'s fighting efficiency, so a prize crew was placed on board with orders to proceed to meet *Altmark. Graf Spee* moved off on her own, with her Arado airworthy again by 12 October. Langsdorff was happy to have his air reconnaissance back as, on the following day, his radio monitors reported a great increase in Allied wireless traffic on the African coast. He feared his presence had indeed been discovered and that this might lead both to a British build-up on the African coast and the institution of convoy. The departure of units of the Mediterranean Fleet had been reported and, over-pessimistically, Langsdorff calculated he might soon be facing in the South Atlantic the battleship *Malaya*, the carriers *Glorious* and *Eagle*, and the heavy cruisers *Cumberland* and *Exeter*, reinforced by *Norfolk*, *Shropshire*, *Sussex* and *Dorsetshire*, together with six light cruisers.

This tendency to think the worst about possible British movements once his presence had been made known was a feature of Langsdorff's mentality. These forces could search the area St Helena–Ascension–Trinidad, as well as the sea routes northwards from the Plate and Cape–Freetown. He thought enemy warships were likely to be based at St Helena and Ascension as well as Cape Town and Freetown. Langsdorff therefore decided to refuel and take on stores from *Altmark* as soon as possible, sink *Huntsman* and move his waiting area west. *Graf Spee* met up with *Altmark* on 14 October at 21°59' S, 15°02' W. The armoured ship's disguise was so effective that the auxiliary, disguised as the Norwegian tanker *Sogne*, thought for a moment that she had been caught by an enemy warship. The ship was preparing for scuttling when signals from *Graf Spee* put the jittery auxiliary crew at their ease.

After fuelling, the two ships moved to meet *Huntsman*, rendezvous being made on the morning of 16 October at 16°11' S, 17°06' W. The British ship was moored alongside *Altmark* and two days were spent transferring stores and part of *Huntsman*'s cargo to the German supply ship. Eighty tons' worth were sent straight on by boat to *Graf Spee*. Langsdorff also decided to turn his auxiliary into a prison ship, both to lessen pressure on his own spaces and, he thought, to give *Altmark* some protection if she were found by an enemy ship. This was unfortunate for the merchant seamen as Kapitän K.H. Dau, *Altmark*'s commanding officer, had an abiding hatred of the British dating back to his captivity in Britain during the First World War. Relations were bad between Dau and his prisoners, although some of the more generous-minded of them later said that at least some of the privations they faced – an ordeal that became legendary as British propaganda made the most of it – derived from putting so many recalcitrant personnel into spaces in a vessel never designed to act as a P.O.W. ship.

The extended replenishment allowed a self-maintenance period for *Graf Spee*, and her engineers overhauled the diesels. Langsdorff now considered his next moves. Berlin had signalled him on the 16th with a situation report as to the movement of enemy ships. The news was mixed. A French squadron had been formed around the fast battleship *Strasbourg* and was on its way to Dakar. However, *Malaya* and *Glorious* were reassuringly far away at Aden. Other good news was that of U-boat ace Günther Prien's success in torpedoing the British battleship *Royal Oak* in Scapa Flow. This must have made Langsdorff even more frustrated at the restrictive orders that precluded him from achieving similar success on the high seas. He had to keep out of the reported hunting groups' way and he had to avoid convoys with even the lightest escort. He knew from *Huntsman* that the Cape route was thought safe by the Allies. The best option to find unprotected shipping therefore was to go south to exploit the opportunities the

Cape offered. He wanted to continue commerce raiding as long as possible, both to disrupt Allied shipping and to force the deployment of disproportionate Allied forces in its defence. Given the state of *Graf Spee*'s engines and refrigeration plant, as well as the availability of supplies, he planned to break back to Germany in the new moon period of January 1940. *Huntsman* was scuttled with explosive charges and *Graf Spee* moved off to the south east to find ships sailing along the routes detailed in the documents found in the British ships.

Langsdorff was rewarded at 13.20 hrs on 22 October, off Walvis Bay, by the 5,299 ton *Trevanion*, bound from Australia to the UK. *Graf Spee* approached, as usual, head-on; but, when close, turned and ran up the ensign. She signalled to the merchantman not to use the radio, but Captain J.M. Edwards calmly told his Radio Officer, N.C Martinson, to send an R.R.R. message. *Graf Spee* opened fire with one of her 20-mm guns. As the shaken radio operator paused, firing stopped; undeterred, Edwards insisted Martinson continue. Again *Graf Spee* opened fire, but the message was completed, albeit with a mistaken position. The 20-mm rounds shattered the bridge; miraculously, no one was wounded. Edwards was able under fire to put his confidential documents over the side in the weighted bag before the armed boarding party took control of the ship. Aboard the Panzerschiff, with typical courtesy, Langsdorff congratulated Edwards on his gallantry. *Trevanion* was scuttled with two bombs by the boarding party at 19°40' S, 4°02' E.[14]

The R.R.R. was received by the merchantman *Llanstephan Castle* and passed on to the Royal Navy at Freetown. Langsdorff had to assume it had been received and he therefore needed to move away. A signal from Raeder the same day *Trevanion* was sunk suggested the Indian Ocean, but left things to Langsdorff. The latter's mind was working along the same lines. His E.S.M. crew were picking up numerous indications of British activity, including a comforting signal that a U-boat had been sighted, coincidentally in *Graf Spee*'s position at the time. The confusion created by this error gave the real threat useful cover; but *Graf Spee*'s Arado reported a merchantman on the 23rd, and although it was never found, Langsdorff worried that the truth of *Graf Spee*'s presence might have been revealed after all.

Berlin was also worried about their ships being spotted from the air and, on 24 October, moved *Altmark* six hundred miles further west. Thus, it was not until the morning of 28 October that *Graf Spee* and *Altmark* made a rendezvous at 26°37' S, 17°49' W. After taking on fuel and transferring *Trevanion*'s prisoners, Langsdorff made off eastwards round the Cape and into the Indian Ocean to attack shipping south of Madagascar.

Part of Langsdorff's logic was to give the impression of raider activity in the Indian Ocean, creating confusion and diverting attention, before his engines forced him to return home. His hard-pressed engineers had done some useful self-maintenance between the 24th and the 29th, but Langsdorff knew he could not put off a dockyard overhaul beyond January 1940. This return home in the New Year was announced to the crew on 30 October, along with the uplifting news that a hundred Iron Crosses had been awarded to the ship's company. The weather, good at first, worsened; straining the poor seakeeping qualities of the Panzerschiff design. For two days, *Graf Spee* had to heave-to. The heavy seas south of the Cape prevented both boarding operations and the use of the seaplane; further raiding was out of the question. Langsdorff therefore decided to proceed to the calmer waters around Mozambique, where he would raid as the *Graf Spee*. He would then return to Latin American waters as the *Scheer* before making back to Germany.

By 8 November the sea was calm enough to use the seaplane; but nothing was sighted, and, on the Arado's return, it was found that its spare engine was also cracking. It was repairable, but its flying hours were severely numbered. *Graf Spee* prowled first to the East of Madagascar but, finding no victims, moved into the Mozambique channel. There would normally have been ships carrying wool from Australia, but the shearing had been delayed that year and the ships had not yet sailed. In his frustration, Langsdorff considered using up the Arado's few remaining hours in a bombing raid on the oil tanks at

Durban but decided against it as it might lead to his being found. He closed the Mozambiquean coast near Laurenço Marques, where he found a small neutral Dutch ship after nightfall on the 14th. Langsdorff was by now desperate enough to make his presence felt by boarding a neutral, but high seas prevented it.

A little better luck was to be had the following day when the 706-ton coastal tanker *Africa Shell* was spotted, hugging the coast to take advantage of neutral Portuguese waters. Langsdorff saw free fuel and decided to go for the small prize. In the event, *Africa Shell* was a petrol carrier supporting the Empire passenger flying boats on the South Africa run; she was also in ballast, having discharged her last cargo. She was boarded and her master, Captain Patrick Dove, captured. The crew were allowed to row ashore and the empty ship was then sunk. Before she had slipped beneath the waves, a Japanese ship hove into view. *Graf Spee* did nothing about her but sailed away in a north-easterly direction to put any trackers off the scent before turning south-eastwards again.

Langsdorff now decided he had at least created some confusion in the Indian Ocean. His E.S.M. equipment picked up an Allied signal on 16 November from Senior Naval Officer Durban, warning of the presence of a German raider. This was reported by Langsdorff back to Berlin, along with his intention to rejoin *Altmark* in the South Atlantic. *Graf Spee*'s captain also reiterated his request to be allowed to engage warships. Pending a reply, Langsdorff decided to continue moving south eastwards, stopping a Dutch ship on the 16th but allowing it to proceed. At about midnight he turned to starboard, aiming to head down to latitude 40' for the move round the Cape. Once again, however, *Graf Spee* proved unsuitable for the seas found in the Roaring Forties. Captain Dove later reported: 'From where I stood in the lee of the funnel, I could see that *Graf Spee* was making a beast of herself, as we say in the service. She was pitching and rolling, heavy seas were breaking sheer across her, and time after time she buried her foredeck in solid green seas right over her forward gun turret.'[15]

On 23 November a major overhaul of engines began, as she cruised at reduced speed on only part of her diesel outfit. *Graf Spee* had run 30,000 nautical miles since leaving Germany and pistons required changing. Cracks to the auxiliary motors had also to be attended to. As his ship sailed slowly into deserted waters, Langsdorff now made some crucial decisions, decisions that were to seal the fate both of his ship – and of himself.

CHAPTER THREE

Bending the Rules

Some time after the event, Captain Dove recalled a conversation with his most civil captor as they strolled along *Graf Spee*'s deck. 'You see', Langsdorff had said, 'there can be no Coronel or Falkland Islands for me. I must not stay and fight British ships. My orders are to sink your merchant boats and disappear again. Often I have difficulty in explaining to my officers that I am not a coward, but that we have a particular kind of work to do. These men are trained to fight and they do not care too much for this sort of warfare.'[1]

By 24 November 1939, Langsdorff's patience had run out. At noon he called an officers' meeting. He told them first that *Graf Spee* was going home to Germany. He then dropped his bombshell. As Oberleutnant Rasenack, the assistant gunnery officer, reported it, Langsdorff went on: 'From today onwards, contrary to the tactical plan employed so far, we will not avoid enemy ships but will meet them and will sink anything that comes within range of our guns, even at the risk of losing the ship'.[2] Langsdorff seemingly felt not only that action should be risked, but that a notable victory was a necessity in these waters; as it was far from certain that another German ship would appear in the region, at least for some time. He now wanted another Coronel to add still greater lustre to the *Graf Spee* name, a Coronel this time without a Falklands.

Langsdorff knew the enormity of what he was doing. On 26

November, *Graf Spee* met *Altmark* for a final replenishment at 25° S, 9°58' W. As the two ships began the process of revictualling, restoring and refuelling, Langsdorff wrote a long, nine-page section in the war diary rehearsing the reasons for this crucial – also highly insubordinate and risky – decision.

He began by analysing the state of his ship, stressing that its armament had no deficiencies – despite *Graf Spee* having travelled 30,000 miles. When replenishment was complete he would have 2,841 tons of diesel oil on board, enough to allow *Graf Spee* to remain at sea for three more months. *Altmark* had 3,600 tons extra aboard. The next section he headed 'Decision for the Continuation of the Operation'. The first part of this referred to 'Operational Orders and Further Instructions of the Seekriegsleitung (Naval War Command)'. He first rehearsed the orders under which he had been operating:

> *Graf Spee* is to inflict damage on enemy trade in as long and sustained a manner as possible, and at least to disturb it, to tie down as many forces as possible in commerce protection.
>
> In explanation of this task, the Seekriegsleitung issued the instruction to ensure during operations that the enemy should not achieve a prestige success by early elimination of the Panzerschiffe and that the 'full commitment' ('*voller Einsatz*') of the Panzerschiffe should be avoided.
>
> Given the exceptionally good conditions of visibility in the South Atlantic, this means a tactic designed to make it more difficult for the enemy to establish contact with cruisers. Since the range of visibility during the day and on moonlit nights as a rule extended beyond the range of one's weapons, there was little prospect of shaking off a faster shadower.
>
> The Panzerschiff therefore left its operational area every time it was certain that the enemy was alarmed and had obtained some indication of the position of the ship. Engagements were to be avoided because, even after victorious battle, hits that were in themselves insignificant might result in a shortening of the commerce war.

> The condition of the engines demands an overhaul in dock. It had already been suggested from here on 23 October that this should be scheduled for January 1940. The time of commerce war is therefore in any case nearing its end.[3]

So far Raeder would have been happy to read the document, and the early part was clearly intended to soften him up by demonstrating Langsdorff's clear understanding of the logic of the naval command's raiding strategy. The C-in-C would, however, have been most unhappy with the continuation of paragraph five:

> It is therefore not as necessary as in the past to account for the possibility that the ship might be hit. When *Graf Spee* approaches target range, it can be expected that the powerful artillery of the Panzerschiff can at least damage any anticipated enemy, except for the *Renown*, to such an extent that it is rendered ineffective as a shadower, and on the other hand that the hits that are to be expected cannot significantly impair the return journey.

Engagement with warships was therefore no longer to be avoided. Langsdorff conceded that the clear moonlit nights of the South Atlantic still prevented decisive action in darkness or shaking off a fast shadower after nightfall. The circumstances, however, dictated a more aggressive approach by day:

> It is precisely because *Graf Spee* is disappearing from the South Atlantic and it cannot be foreseen when a second commerce raider can operate here that it must be perceived to have achieved an objectively significant success before leaving the area.

The captain then assessed his 'Results So Far'. Measured by tonnage actually sunk, the *Graf Spee*'s commerce war could not be decisive in the war as a whole. This was not to be expected, given the commitment of only one ship, and given 'English behaviour'. However, he went on:

> In the context of other successes (U-boats and mines) these sinkings nevertheless contribute to undermining before the world the English claim to unlimited command of the sea.

Their indirect effects, Langsdorff argued, were even more important:

> Due to the deployment of the Panzerschiffe, the enemy has taken very far-reaching protective measures and to this end has used forces, which exceed ours many times. He has completely secured individual routes such as the Colombo–Aden route by using battleships and aircraft carriers, (and) in others increased the risk for Panzerschiffe operating according to prize rules. As far as is currently discernible, he has, however, not attempted to search those sea areas in which German commerce raiders have to replenish during pauses in operations.
>
> The enemy has largely gone over to convoys and has to accept the inherent disadvantages.[4]

Langsdorff finished by describing his immediate plans. He would complete his machinery overhaul and then, until 6 December, he would operate against the Cape route around where he had sunk *Trevanion*. Then, depending on the state of his diesels, he would return home or have a final lunge against the River Plate traffic. *Altmark* would take up a suitable waiting position to cover either of these options.

One can detect in these pages the trend of Langsdorff's thought. He would bend the rules rather than totally go against them. If convoys were likely because of the British adoption of them, then there might be opportunities for action against warships within the terms of his original orders that allowed: 'engagements... if this furthers the main purpose of the operation'. Minor damage would be acceptable in the context of an imminent return home. Crucially, Langsdorff had fallen for the 'pocket battleship' myth by grossly overestimating the capacity of his ship, both to damage opponents quickly and effectively and to take damage without compromising seaworthiness.

The wardroom officers generally approved of their captain's insubordination, although they may have been unaware that the change in tactics was not authorised. Rasenack said that he had been displeased for some time with the tactics of avoiding action, although: 'They were the most reasonable for the accomplishment of our mission. Come what may! That was for me the best directive. It would be a pity if we had to return to our fatherland without our guns having received their baptism of fire. A cruiser or some ship not superior to us would be a fine target for our guns and a fine finale to our cruise.'[5]

Langsdorff now disguised his ship much more completely than before. This was perhaps primarily to increase her chances of surprising merchantmen; but Langsdorff may have had in mind closing a warship in order to surprise and sink, or seriously damage, her. Certainly, much effort was expended. It was decided to convert *Graf Spee* into a passable impression of a British battlecruiser or French cruiser. A false gun turret was built on top of the conning tower and lower bridge. Two false gun barrels of exactly the correct size were made. They were given supports so they would not droop, but these thin posts were invisible at a distance and the result was quite convincing. A second 'funnel' was built on the after gunnery control position, abaft the seaplane catapult. The hull of the ship was

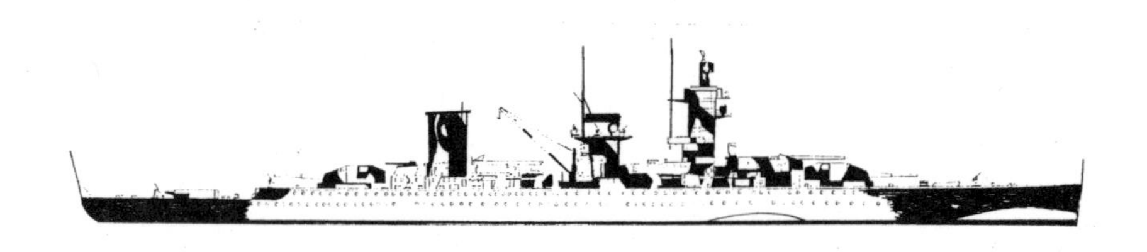

Graf Spee disguised as an Allied battlecruiser. Note the false gun turret and high-speed 'bow wave' design.

repainted in a British shade of grey with camouflaged superstructure to confuse the ship's silhouette as much as possible. False bow and midship waves were also painted on the ship to make more difficult distant estimates of speed for fire control purposes. By the evening of 28 November the work was complete, and Langsdorff, Fregattenkapitän Paul Ascher, *Graf Spee*'s gunnery officer, and Rasenack took a boat round the ship to inspect their handiwork. They were all very pleased with the results.

The following day, *Graf Spee* and *Altmark* parted company after the former had used the latter as a 'target' to adjust her fire control instruments. Langsdorff decided to risk using the Arado, which had for some time been painted in deceptive markings, to conduct a search. The aircraft successfully completed the mission, although it sighted nothing. On 2 December, the Arado was launched again and flew off to the south. Then, smoke was spotted in the opposite direction; the masthead rangefinder gave a reading of 53 km, testimony both to the power of the Zeiss stereoscopic equipment and the clear South Atlantic conditions. The ship was the *Doric Star*, a 10,086 ton Blue Star line refrigerated cargo liner, built in 1921, carrying a cargo of sheep meat, cheese and butter from New Zealand to UK.

Langsdorff was worried about his seaplane and, instead of exploiting his new disguise, ordered *Graf Spee*'s 11-in guns to open fire at extreme range across the bows of the target, whose upperworks were now just visible. *Doric Star*'s first inkling of danger was when a large shell sent up a waterspout a hundred yards away. Captain William Stubbs at once ordered his Radio Officer to make an R.R.R. signal and rang for full-speed. A second heavy shell soon demonstrated he could not get away, so *Doric Star* stopped engines while still transmitting an amplified signal mentioning a 'battleship'. The German lamp signals to stop the radio were at first ignored; but, when the Radio Officer reported his message had been repeated by other ships, Stubbs gave in to *Graf Spee*'s threat to open fire if signals did not cease. Armed only with a 12-pdr anti-submarine gun aft, resistance was out of the question.

Stubbs had considered scuttling his ship and his valuable cargo; and even when he submitted to boarding, he was able to use subterfuge to prevent the Germans capturing the valuable food. He insisted the ship was carrying only wool and the German physical search of the cargo was only cursory, as by now the Germans had received a distress call from the Arado. Its batteries were defective and the aircrew had not heard about the mother ship's change of course. It had landed in heavy open seas and sustained damage to a float; help was urgently required. Langsdorff considered taking *Doric Star* as a prize but her Chief Engineer had wrecked the engines. Once her crew had been taken off, the big ship was sunk by *Graf Spee* with all three weapons available: explosive charges, gunfire and a torpedo.

If Langsdorff had really wanted to reveal his presence, he had succeeded. His E.S.M. crew reported that six ships had repeated the R.R.R., including a warship. *Graf Spee* now sped off to towards the seaplane's emergency beacon; and, in the increasing gloom, spotted the Arado's visual signal. The aircraft was picked up safely. Langsdorff's concerns had apparently led him into making a serious error that gave away his position. It was, however, no mistake. Langsdorff's new attitude to action meant that, at the very least, he was willing to take what would previously have been unreasonable risks. If a warship had been alerted, so much the worse for her; she would be ambushed by the disguised *Graf Spee*, and a new and glorious chapter added to the history of the Kriegsmarine!

****

Graf Spee cruised south-westward during the night and in the dawn light spotted smoke on the port quarter. The German closed at full speed, and at 20 km, a merchant ship hove into sight. Once she had closed the merchantman the *Graf Spee* turned broadside on, exchanged the French flag for a German one and signalled her to stop. She was the 7,983 ton Furness Withy ship *Tairoa*, bound for UK from Australia with a cargo of meat, wool and lead. *Graf Spee* fired a shot across her bows and signalled *Tairoa* to stop. Captain W.B.S. Starr then ordered the Radio Officer, P.J. Cummins, to make an R.R.R. that they had been attacked by the *Admiral Scheer* at 21°38' S, 3°13' W. (In fact, *Graf Spee* was currently masquerading as the *Deutschland*.) Langsdorff had decided after his first prize that heavier calibre weapons were required for dissuasive fire, and he now opened up with one of his twin 37-mm guns. Starr had ordered his wireless office to be protected with sandbags but the German shells eventually succeeded in knocking out the radio. For his gallantry in signalling until his equipment was wrecked, Cummins received the MBE. The German fire caused significant destruction and wounded five crew members. The Germans would have liked to take *Tairoa* to *Altmark*, but their fire had damaged the steering gear. The packing of the ship made it difficult to access the food part of the cargo and the Germans had to be satisfied with the contents of the storerooms and pantry. One crucial find, however, were eighteen bottles of carbonic acid for the *Graf Spee*'s defective refrigeration plant. Eventually the 84-strong crew, largely made up of lascars, was taken off and the ship sunk with a torpedo. Langsdorff, typically, congratulated Starr and Cummins on their bravery – which had had some results. *Tairoa*'s desperate message had been picked up, albeit in garbled form, by another ship, the *Port Chalmers* (she had also been a recipient of *Doric Star*'s R.R.R.). The British now had confirmation that a pocket battleship was abroad in the South Atlantic.

Langsdorff now intended to move to South American waters, firstly to the area of Santos Bay, south of Rio; but, before he did so, he felt it desirable to have another replenishment from *Altmark*, where he also wished to deposit the bulk of his prisoners. The ships met up once more on 6 December at 24°27' S, 19°45' W. All prisoners except the Captains and Radio Officers of the sunken merchant ships were transferred to *Altmark*. The German logic was that the officers now knew too much about German methods and their capture on the auxiliary could not be risked. Two Captains, Brown of *Huntsman* and Starr of *Tairoa*, were, however, allowed to accompany their lascar crews on board *Altmark.* The three worst wounded boys from *Tairoa* also stayed in *Graf Spee*'s hospital.

The two German ships continued to move slowly westwards, even as they refuelled. As night fell, Ascher asked for permission to exercise his searchlights using *Altmark* as target. Langsdorff acceded as the waters through which *Graf Spee* was passing were normally deserted. Shortly afterwards, however, an unlit merchantman was spotted to starboard. Langsdorff decided not to attack, despite the fears of his officers that the ship must have seen the lights. At this stage, the Captain did not want to risk another R.R.R. that would give the British early warning of his move westward. He knew from intelligence received from Berlin on the 4th that two 8-in. gun cruisers, *Cumberland* and *Exeter*, and two 6-in. gun ships, *Ajax* and *Achilles,* were patrolling the area from Rio to the Plate. He did not want them to concentrate unnecessarily. He was also told that the battlecruiser *Renown* and the carrier *Ark Royal* were in West African waters, while two heavy cruisers were operating around the Cape.

Graf Spee and *Altmark* split up on 7 December, and the Panzerschiff continued towards the Brazilian coast, At 1746 hrs smoke was sighted and Langsdorff decided to take the offered kill. It was the Harwood Steamship Company's 3,895 ton *Streonshalh*, bound from Montevideo with a cargo of wheat to Freetown to pick up a convoy. *Graf Spee* was able to close to very short range before ordering the ship not to transmit. Captain J.J. Robinson felt he had little choice but to comply, although he did his best to dispose of confidential papers in weighted bags over the side. He tore up his routing instructions and stirred them into a pot of paint. The Germans were however able to find sufficient information on board the ship, not least a copy of the Buenos Aires Herald in the Chief Engineer's cabin, to obtain both the port of origin of the ship and information on sailings from the Plate Estuary. The crew was taken off the doomed ship and it was sent to the bottom by *Graf Spee*'s 4.1-in. guns.

The information in *Streonshalh* attracted Langsdorff once more to the Plate estuary. Some rich pickings had been noted in the newspaper as either being there or having sailed from there recently, notably the 14,000 ton *Highland Monarch* which had sailed only two days previously. Some rough notes had also given an indication of a turning point for shipping, three hundred miles due east of the Plate. Langsdorff decided to make for this invisible point in the sea. He was undeterred by an intelligence report of the presence of the British cruiser *Achilles* in Montevideo. Indeed, other news from Berlin was positively encouraging. Not only the *Highland Monarch*, but the *Andalusia Star* was also sailing from Montevideo. Perhaps even more tempting, a small convoy of four ships of 30,000 tons total protected by an auxiliary cruiser was reported as sailing from the Uruguayan capital. Such a target was a tempting one. Already, Langsdorff knew, the armed merchant cruiser *Rawalpindi* had been sunk by *Scharnhorst* or *Gneisenau* on the Northern patrol. A similar ship would be easy meat for his 11-in. guns. If sinking her did not take too long, the convoy would add enough tonnage to *Graf Spee*'s tally to ensure that she exceeded the total sunk by the *Emden* in the First World War. It would be a fitting finale to the voyage. *Achilles* on her own would also be a tempting and not too difficult target, even if supported by the two destroyers he imagined might also be used for escort purposes. *Graf Spee* was on her way home. In Langsdorff's view, she could now afford to take risks, in accordance with the captain's new policy. With uncharacteristic aggression for a navy whose doctrine was steeped in the principle of 'fleet in being', the German Navy's former flagship was hunting for glory, and the waters off the Plate seemed the best place to find it.

Langsdorff flew off as many searches as his Arado's engine could take; but on 11 December the BMW power unit finally expired, and the seaplane was partially dismantled on the catapult. In circumstances where good situational awareness was more important than at any previous time on the voyage, *Graf Spee* had lost her main long-range reconnaissance platform. Langsdorff also reconsidered his camouflage strategy. The dummy turrets and funnel interfered with his fire control, especially if the ship was to be presented with multiple targets, as might be the case in a convoy action. The disguise was dismantled.

So, partially blinded, but looking more like a Panzerschiff again, *Graf Spee* patrolled the focal point three hundred miles off the Plate. Nothing was found, nothing that is until 0552 hrs on the cloudless, clear morning of 13 December when, with the ship moving south eastwards at 155 degrees at 15 knots, at a range of 31,000 metres, two – and then four more – thin masts appeared on the horizon. The bridge informed Langsdorff in his sea cabin and the captain ordered course and speed to be maintained towards the contacts. Here, he assumed, were *Achilles* and the two destroyers covering the notional convoy. On his reaching the bridge, Langsdorff was reminded by the Chief Navigating Officer, Korvettenkapitän Jurgen Wattenberg, of the standing orders, reiterated many times, to avoid action even with inferior enemy forces. There was a brief silence. Perhaps Langsdorff's mind ran one last time through the logic that made an engagement with a convoy escort less a direct disobedience to orders, more a bending of the rules. Thus Langsdorff made his fateful (and fatal) decision. 'I suspect a convoy', he reportedly said. 'The protecting forces will go all out, that will then give a fine target'.[6] Langsdorff ordered the ship to action stations and, before making his way to his chosen combat position in the foretop, pronounced decisively: 'Now we will see!'[7]

Part Two
Duel

CHAPTER FOUR

The Hunters

The three ships Langsdorff was heading towards were HMS *Ajax*, HMS *Achilles* and HMS *Exeter*, three of the four cruisers that made up raider hunting group G under Commodore Henry Harwood, who had been commanding the South American Division of the Royal Navy since 1936. The Allies had received hard information that pocket battleships were at large only on 1 October, when *Clement*'s crew came ashore in South America.[1] Much shipping was already in convoy on the North Atlantic routes because of Lemp's mistaken sinking of the liner *Athenia* giving the British the (for a time, equally mistaken) impression that the Germans had restored unrestricted submarine warfare. This effectively neutralised *Deutschland*, which was covering these routes, bound by the same 'no full commitment' rules that hampered *Graf Spee*. The prototype Panzerschiff sank but two ships, one a neutral Norwegian, and captured a third, another neutral, an American. She was then recalled, arriving back in Germany in mid-November.

On 4 October, the British First Sea Lord, Admiral Sir Dudley Pound, had chaired a meeting on how to deal with the raider or raiders on the trade routes. The meeting rejected convoy in the South Atlantic and Indian Ocean because of a perceived shortage of escorts and unacceptable delays to shipping. The loss rate from the raiders would have to be accepted as 'inevitable'.[2] However, attempts were to be made to attack the raiders by the formation of hunting groups, which played into the Germans' hands. A major aim of raiding operations was to so damage or harass enemy trade that as many Allied forces as possible would have to be employed in commerce protection. The Allies were indeed forced to spread their assets very widely to cope with the threat. No fewer than eight hunting groups were formed:

Force F: two British 8-in. cruisers, *Berwick* and *York*, covering the coast of North America;
Force G: two British 8-in. cruisers, *Cumberland* and *Exeter* covering the eastern coast of South America;
Force H: two British 8-in. cruisers, *Shropshire* and *Sussex* covering the Cape of Good Hope;
Force I: the British carrier *Eagle* and the 8-in. cruisers *Cornwall* and *Dorsetshire* covering waters around Ceylon;
Force K: the British battlecruiser *Renown*, the carrier *Ark Royal* and a 6-in. cruiser covering the area Pernambuco-Freetown;
Force L: a French battle group containing the fast battleship *Dunkerque*, the carrier *Bearn* and the 6-in. cruisers *Gloire*, *Montcalm* and *Georges Leygues* operating out of Brest;
Force M: the French 8-in. cruisers *Dupleix* and *Foch* operating off the African coast out of Dakar;
Force N: the French fast battleship *Strasbourg* and British carrier *Hermes* operating in the West Indies.[3]

Each hunting group was to search in radio silence around areas where trade was 'thick'. Each was deemed capable of destroying either a Panzerschiff or a Hipper class cruiser; but destruction by one force alone was not necessary, as raiders were both far from repair facilities and dependent on their mobility. 'A weaker force, if not able to effect immediate destruct may, by resolute attack, be able to cripple an opponent sufficiently to ensure a certain subsequent location and destruction by other forces.'

The transatlantic convoys had their escorts enlarged by the addition of battleships *Resolution* and *Revenge* and the 6-in. cruisers *Emerald* and *Enterprise.* With independently routed shipping, however, the raider did not have to encounter Allied warships and it was only a matter of luck if they ever came close. German intelligence of British movements at this stage of the war seems to have been better than British knowledge of German. The Admiralty had very little idea what was operating where. All it knew was that there was at least one raider at large, probably a pocket battleship and probably in the Central Atlantic, a view confirmed by *Deutschland*'s first (and only) British kill, the *Stonegate*, sunk six hundred miles east of Bermuda. It took three weeks for more intelligence to be received, when the crew of *Deutschland*'s Norwegian victim were landed in the Orkneys and then the captured American prize, *City of Flint*, arrived at Murmansk, where she had been sent. If nothing else, *Graf Spee*'s elder sister was providing useful cover. The same day, 22 October, news of the *Trevanion* attack off Freetown came in, which fitted the 'lone Atlantic raider' theory. The sinking of the *Rawalpindi* by *Scharnhorst* and *Gneisenau* a month later – that was attributed thanks to misidentification to *Deutschland* – seemed to show the pocket battleship had broken the blockade and returned home.

The only clue that two ships might be at large had come from the released masters of the *Stonegate* and the *Clement*, who said they had been sunk by the *Deutschland* and the *Admiral Scheer* respectively. The Allied groups were later reshuffled, with Forces M and N being reformed as Force X (*Hermes*, *Dupleix* and *Foch*) and Force Y (*Strasbourg* and two 6-in. cruisers) to patrol Dakar-Pernambuco. More strength was also given to the Atlantic convoys in the shape of the battleship *Warspite*, battlecruiser *Repulse* and the carrier *Furious*; while an extra Indian Ocean Group, Force J, was formed of the battleship *Malaya* and the carrier *Glorious*.

Forces G, H and K were placed under the orders of Admiral Sir D'Oyly Lyon, British C-in-C South Atlantic. Force G with its wide beat along the South American coast received welcome reinforcement in the shape of the light cruisers *Ajax* and *Achilles*. *Ajax* was a long-standing member of the South American Division, having been on the station longer than *Exeter*. She had been the sole representative of the Royal Navy on the east coast of South America on the outbreak of war, when she scored perhaps the Royal Navy's first success, the German merchant ship *Olinda*, sunk after her crew had been taken off.[4] When the hunting groups were first formed, she was allocated as the cruiser in Force K but then reverted to Harwood's command. Her sister, the New Zealand-manned *Achilles*, joined the South Atlantic station from the Pacific through the Straits of Magellan, arriving at the Falkland Islands on 22 October. Four days later, *Achilles* rendezvoused with Harwood's flagship, the heavy cruiser *Exeter*, and the two ships manœuvred together for the first time.

The arrival of *Achilles* allowed Harwood the following day to send *Exeter*, his home since appointment in 1936, to the Falklands for a rest and self-refit. His broad pendant was transferred to *Ajax*. The known sinkings in late October and November both drew Forces H and K to waters around the Cape and eventually allowed Harwood to join *Exeter* at Port Stanley to rest and refit, leaving *Cumberland* covering the Plate and *Achilles*, Rio. Harwood was acutely conscious of the salience of 8 December as the anniversary of the Falkland Islands battle. In case the German pocket battleship tried to attack Port Stanley that day, he decided to relieve *Cumberland* with his flagship and concentrate his heavy cruisers in the Falklands on the 7th. In any case, *Cumberland* was much in need of a refit and after two days patrolling the islands she was to enter Port Stanley to begin.

The very day *Ajax* left Port Stanley, 2 December, Harwood received news of the *Doric Star* attack. Before dawn the following day he had news of another unknown casualty (*Tairoa*) to the south west of *Doric Star*'s position. Harwood mulled the matter over on the morning of the 3rd, using a message pad as a decision aid (see illustration on p. 53). On the right, he put the raider's position on the afternoon of the 4th. Then he drew a line north westwards to a point it might reach on the 8th. He then drew three lines, one up to the focal area off Rio, one across to the focal area off the Plate and one down to the Falklands. He calculated on the top of the form how far a pocket battleship might steam in six days, at a cruising speed of fifteen knots. From this, he estimated that the German ship might reach Rio by the forenoon of December 12th, the Plate by the morning of the 13th or the Falkland Islands by the 14th. Which one would it be? All Harwood's long experience of the station went into his next judgment. He probably also remembered *Exeter*'s visit to New York in 1939 for the World's Fair; Harwood's wife, Joan, had great difficulty in drawing him away from a map of shipping movements in South American waters that clearly showed the Plate as the major focal point. He put an arrow on the line by the 'P' on his pad.[5] As he said in his dispatch: 'I decided that the Plate, with its larger number of ships and its very valuable grain and meat trade, was the vital area to be defended. I therefore arranged to concentrate there my available

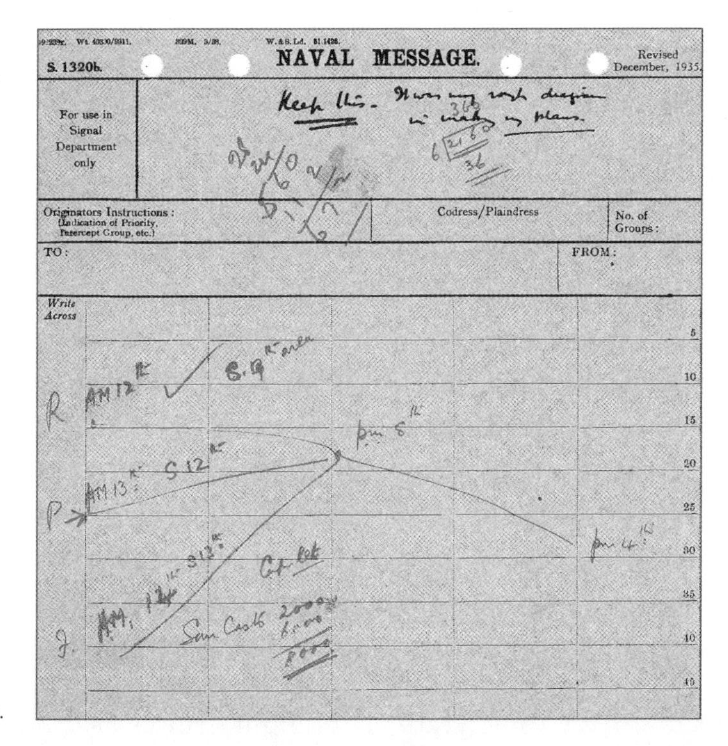
S. 1320b. NAVAL MESSAGE. Revised December, 1935.

For use in Signal Department only

Keep this. It was my rough diagram in making my plans.

Originators Instructions: (Indication of Priority, Intercept Group, etc.)

Codress/Plaindress

No. of Groups:

TO:

FROM:

Write Across

R AM 12th

P AM 13th

pm 8th

pm 4th

The famous Harwood 'doodle', predicting *Graf Spee*'s arrival off the River Plate on a.m. 13 December, 1939.

forces in advance of the time it was anticipated the Raider might start operations in that area.'[6]

Harwood worked out how far *Cumberland* could steam in a day at 28 knots, 672 miles and added up how much oil two tankers, *Capulet* and *San Castro*, bound for the Falklands, could bring him if he had to spend any amount of time off the Plate.[7] At 1315 hrs on 3 December, Harwood made a signal to his Division. *Cumberland* was to continue her self-refit but would keep two of her four shafts at short notice. *Achilles* was to leave Rio to arrive and fuel at Montevideo early on the morning of 8 December. The following day, *Exeter* was to leave the Falklands for the Plate. *Ajax* and *Achilles* were to concentrate at 35° S., 50° W. on the afternoon of the 10th. *Exeter* was to move north and pass 150 miles directly off the Medanos lighthouse at 0700 hrs on the 12th. If the three cruisers had not rendezvoused with *Exeter* by that time, further instructions would be issued. Strict wireless silence was to be kept. The die was cast.

****

Henry Harwood Harwood, 'Bobby' Harwood as he was more generally known, was older than Langsdorff, having been born on 19 January 1888. He was one of the last cadets entered under the old Britannia scheme, joining a static training ship in the River Dart in 1903, aged fifteen. He was an able young man, gaining straight first-class passes in his lieutenant's examination. Harwood chose the most demanding specialisation, intellectually, that of a torpedo officer (which at that time covered all electrical matters also). His long course at HMS Vernon, the torpedo school at Portsmouth, and at the Royal Naval College, Greenwich, lasted from 1911 to 1913. During the First World War, he served as torpedo officer, first in the armoured cruiser *Sutlej* and then in the new battleship *Royal Sovereign* in which he was promoted Lieutenant Commander. His first experience of the South American Station came in 1919 when he became Fleet Torpedo Officer for three years in the light cruiser *Southampton.* Harwood learned Spanish, travelled widely in South America and became very interested both in the region in general and its naval aspects.[8]

His next ship was *Southampton*'s sister ship *Dartmouth.* First Lieutenant, Harwood was not long in this cruiser, as the summer of 1921 saw his rapid promotion to Commander. He joined the Staff Course at Greenwich, at which he did well, qualifying for work in the Plans Division on the newly reformed, and much more effective, postwar Naval Staff at the Admiralty. After this, he went to the Mediterranean Fleet – first as senior torpedo officer on the staff of the second-in-command, and then as Fleet Torpedo Officer. Commander Harwood was then appointed as executive officer in the cruiser *Cumberland*, building at Barrow. He took the new ship on its first commission to the China station. Harwood had been a great success as a Commander and, at the end of 1928, was promoted Captain.

His first appointment in the new rank was to the destroyer leader *Warwick* in command of a division of the Fifth Destroyer Flotilla in the Atlantic Fleet. In 1931, Harwood attended the Imperial Defence College before commanding the cruiser HMS *London* in the Mediterranean. The ship was flagship of the Second Cruiser Squadron and the post also carried the duties of Chief Staff Officer to the squadron. Harwood's qualities as a staff officer led to his appointment to the staff of the Senior Officer's War Course at Greenwich from 1934 to 1936. During this time, the reflective Harwood developed in his lectures innovative tactics to deal with the new pocket battleships. He explained to his courses how the best method would be to use separated divisions of cruisers that would force the enemy to split his fire, or engage only one division at a time. There was a general development of British doctrine at this time emphasising divisional rather than linear tactics, and Harwood was at the forefront of its application.[9] Had he but known, by taking on *Exeter*, Hans Langsdorff was facing the Royal Navy's leading expert on the precise tactical doctrine to deal with his ship; and on the regional political circumstances which were later to arise.

In 1936, Harwood received the perfect appointment for an officer of his background: Commodore commanding the South American Division of the South Atlantic Station, flying his broad pendant commanding the heavy cruiser *Exeter*, and operating with the light cruiser *Ajax*. He renewed his love affair with the region and built further on the foundations of a decade and a half before. He took every opportunity further to improve his knowledge of his area, both political and tactical. Fatefully, the first port visited by Harwood in *Exeter* was Montevideo. This was a regular haunt of the cruiser on her flag waving duties, and Harwood's relations with the Uruguayan navy were cordial. On one occasion, he had asked the commander of the gunboat *Uruguay* to act as an enemy ship taking refuge in the Plate in an exercise to improve his knowledge of those waters. The positive effect of Harwood and his ships on opinion in the South Americans was profound. As Harwood's successor in command of *Exeter* wrote after the battle: 'There is no doubt whatever that the presence of *Exeter* and the innumerable friendships made by her officers and men in these States has in no small degree moulded their sentiment towards the Nation'.[10]

Bobby Harwood was a genuinely charming and modest man with a ready smile, clear voice and notably bushy eyebrows. A devout, but not ostentatious, Roman Catholic and a devoted family man (his two sons became highly successful officers in the Royal Navy) he shared the interests of his generation of Naval officers, loving shooting, fishing, golf and gardening. He impressed his contemporaries. Admiral Sir John Edelsten remembered him as: 'a man of parts, possessing a very good brain, very thorough and with great powers of concentration. He was ever ready to take responsibility and I never saw him rattled. He combined these qualities with a love of sport and no one could ever have wished for a more cheerful shipmate'.[11] He got on well with, and inspired respect in, his subordinates also. The commanding officer of *Ajax*, later Admiral Sir Charles Woodhouse, remembered him as a kind and helpful senior officer, always willing to give both a sympathetic hearing and sound advice to a less experienced commander assailed by the doubts and difficulties of a new job (*Ajax* was Woodhouse's first command). Woodhouse also stressed Harwood's professional depth and interest in his theatre of operations. Harwood was: 'constantly considering the special problems with which the South America division would be faced in war, and thinking out the best means of dealing with every foreseeable contingency'. Significantly, like Nelson, Harwood took great pains to imbue his doctrine in his subordinates. Apart from seeing to the fighting efficiency of his ships, Woodhouse recalled, Harwood: 'Took endless trouble to explain to all those whose understanding co-operation would be required in emergency the measures which he anticipated would be necessary'. An able ambassador, both for his service and his country, in Woodhouse's view: 'he had a gift for winning the confidence and esteem of all he met, whether leading government officials or British residents in South America'.[12] Langsdorff could hardly have picked a more formidable opponent.

Concentration occurred as planned on the morning of Tuesday 12 December, and the three cruisers proceeded together to 32° S., 47° W., a position chosen as the most congested part of the diversionary shipping routes, where Harwood expected the pocket battleship might do most damage. He also considered how he could do most damage to it. As he later wrote to his wife: 'A raider is thousands of miles from his base. Attack him, make him use his ammunition. Hit him and he can't repair his damage without going in and risking internment. Reduce his efficiency, upset the moral (sic) of his crew – he is thus weaker. Some other unit can come later and dispose of him. It is not necessary to sink a raider, lovely of course to do so, lame him is most valuable. It is a combination of all these reasons that makes it essential to attack . . .'[13]

At 1200 hrs on the 12th, he made a crucial signal to his force. 'My policy with three cruisers in company versus one Pocket Battleship. Attack at once by day or night. By day act as two units, 1st Division (*Ajax* and *Achilles*) and *Exeter* diverged to permit flank marking. First Division will concentrate gunfire'.[14] If the enemy was found at night, ships were to remain in company in open order until *Ajax* signalled Z.M.M.. This was a variant on the standard signal M.M., ordering commanders of divisions to turn their units to a particular course starting with the rear division. Z.M.M. did the same but for individual ships. The object was to surprise the enemy, forming a line behind the rearmost cruiser crossing the pocket battleship's stern The new leading ship was to lead the line without further orders to maintain decisive gun range. Harwood exercised this manœuvre on the evening of 12 December.

It was a comment on the doctrinal state of the Royal Navy in 1939 that such flexible tactics could be so easily developed and carried out. Although Harwood made it his business to get to know his captains, he had only just met Captain W.E. Parry of *Achilles* on 26 October. There was no need for a special meeting on 12 December; better to have an exercise. All three captains knew what their Commodore expected. The fleet had spent virtually the entire inter-war period learning the lessons of the previous war and the failures of its less than successful, rigid tactical style. In such a situation, a captain like Parry could rapidly become a member of a new 'band of brothers' of likeminded officers scattered over the globe, capable of a hitherto unknown degree of tactical suppleness to outmanœuvre opponents, some of whom might have superior individual strength.

Parry was himself a gifted officer. He was a year older than Langsdorff but had entered the navy earlier under the Selborne scheme as the Dreadnought era dawned. He did well under training, specialised in torpedo work and was promoted captain in 1934. In 1936–7 he commanded HMS *Osprey*, the anti-submarine school at Portland. He then attended the Imperial Defence College before being sent to the New Zealand Division of the Royal Navy to command one of its two cruisers.

Captain Charles Woodhouse of *Ajax* had, like Parry, attended the new Naval Colleges at Osborne and Dartmouth. He had been in action in these waters before serving as a sub-lieutenant in the light cruiser *Bristol* at the battle of the Falkland Islands in 1914. Like Parry also, he would rise to flag rank. His gunnery officer, Lt Cdr. Desmond Dreyer, who would become an Admiral himself, found Woodhouse a 'bit dour', but he was 'much respected' and ran a happy ship.

Exeter's new commanding officer, Captain F.S. Bell, had taken over the ship from Harwood during a curtailed paying-off visit to Plymouth in August 1939. He was another Selborne scheme product who had served in the battleship *Canada* at Jutland, He then served in submarines for a while and, as a Commander, was put on the directing staff of the Staff College in 1932. He was second-in-command of the battlecruiser *Repulse* from 1935 to 1938 when he was promoted Captain.

In all, Harwood's captains were an impressive group. His ships were the products of the attempts made by the inter-war Admiralty to produce cruisers that could be afforded in sufficient numbers to protect the globally spread shipping of the British Empire. The Washington Treaty had created problems in this regard by setting maximum cruiser tonnage at 10,000 tons and gun calibre at 8-in. Rather than being a maximum not to be exceeded this became a new standard to be attained, greatly increasing the cost of individual cruisers and thus making the maintenance of sufficient numbers difficult. If the other naval powers built Washington cruisers, however, Britain would have to follow suit to provide powerful enough platforms to fight them if necessary. The British Empire built thirteen large and impressive three-funnelled County class ships in the 1920s – *Cumberland* was one of the first batch – but only over the increasingly strident complaints of the Treasury; especially when the latter office of state was headed by Chancellor of the Exchequer, Winston Churchill, who (Beatty had said) had gone 'economy mad'.[15] Churchill argued that such cruisers were unnecessary as their only potential opponent with similar ships at the time was Japan and there would 'never be a war with that country in his lifetime'. At the Chancellor's insistence, in 1928 the 'no war for ten years' rule was made a rolling, year-on-year planning assumption. At the same time, the Admiralty, to please the Treasury, laid down the second of two rather smaller 'B'-Type cruisers that did not burden the programme quite so much. The first, laid down the previous year, had been named *York*. The new ship was called *Exeter*. A projected third ship, a sister to *Exeter*, never materialised.

Exeter thus comprised a separate class in herself, being rather different from *York*. Like the Counties, she was armed with 8-in. guns, but only six as against eight in the bigger ships. There were two twin turrets forward and one aft controlled by a director control tower on top of a newly designed, streamlined bridge. The director, with its 15-foot rangefinder, pointed at the target, measuring its range and bearing; but the guns were 'aimed off' by the analogue computer, Admiralty Fire Control Table Mk III, down in the Transmitting Station, protected by 1-in. armour. The table was fed with the position, course and speed of the enemy ship and worked out where it would be when the shells fell. The deflection was sent automatically to the guns, fired on the order 'shoot!' from the Gunnery Officer, that was transmitted by microphone to the Petty Officer at the director sight after firing gongs had sounded to demonstrate that the fire control solution was complete. He pressed a trigger as his sights came 'on'. There was a smaller director aft. If centralised control failed, the turrets, which had their own rangefinders, could revert to local control. The 8-in. guns that could elevate up to 50 degrees fired 256-lb shells out to 30,650 yards. Each gun could fire once every ten seconds. Both semi-armour-piercing capped (S.A.P.C.) shells with 11.5 lb bursting charges, and some high-effect shells with double the charge, were carried. Secondary armament and anti-aircraft protection was provided by four single 4-in. guns with their own high-angle control director aft by the mainmast. *Exeter* also carried two triple 21-in. torpedo tubes, one on each side amidships.[16]

Like *York*, *Exeter* was more heavily armoured than the Counties, with a short 3-in. belt protecting her machinery spaces, 1.5-in. armoured decks above and 3.5-in bulkheads. The ammunition spaces were in an armoured box with 5.5-in. to 3-in. sides, a 3-in. deck and 3-in. bulkheads. This was thicker protection than *Graf Spee*'s, albeit more concentrated. The turrets, however, had only 1-in. protection. Although the ship had two funnels (to help eliminate back draughts), her engines were as in the Counties, with eight boilers and four shaft-geared turbines of 80,000 horsepower; she could make 32 knots. The cruiser was 575-feet overall and 20.25-feet in beam, and her standard displacement was 8,390 tons. *Exeter* was quite a powerful ship and proved to be remarkably tough under fire. She had been launched at Devonport Dockyard on 18 July 1929, and was commissioned on 23 July 1931. She became a familiar sight in South American waters as she had been Harwood's flagship during his entire peacetime period of command.

After *Exeter*, it had been planned to revert to a modification of the County class but these two ships, to be named *Northumberland* and *Surrey*, were cancelled by the new Labour government in 1929. The Admiralty had never given up on the idea of reverting to smaller and cheaper 6-in. armed cruisers, which were, in any case, deemed more suitable than the larger ships to act as scouts with the fleet. While a new design was being prepared, the London Treaty of 1930 effectively placed a cap on numbers of 8-in. armed heavy cruisers and further encouraged the construction of 6-in. light cruisers. Construction of the name ship of a new light cruiser class, *Leander*, began in September 1930. Three more were laid down in 1931 and a fifth in 1933, once the worst of the 1931 financial crisis was over. One of the 1931 ships was HMS *Achilles*, laid down on 11 June at Cammell Lairds, Birkenhead. She was launched on 1 September 1932 and commissioned on 6 October 1933. The final ship was *Ajax*, laid down at Vickers' Barrow yard on 7 February 1933. She was launched on 1 March 1934 and commissioned on 12 April 1935.

The Leanders were designed to a displacement of 7,154 tons although individual ships displaced slightly different amounts as welding was used to a greater extent to reduce weight. *Achilles* displaced 7,030 tons and *Ajax* 6.840. They were armed with eight 6-in. guns in four twin turrets. The guns were of a new Mk XXIII type and were hand-loaded with a maximum rate of fire of one shell every

8–9 seconds. The guns were directed by a single director control tower connected to a T.S. and its A.F.C.T. No back-up was fitted to save money, the original cost of the ships, £1.64 million, being considered high enough in the depressed, early 1930s. Deleting the back-up director saved £44,000. Instead an austere, non-revolving control position was fitted aft with receivers for instruments in other parts of the ship and a spotting telescope. Standard shells were 112 lb. semi-armour-piercing, known as C.P.B.C., Common Pointed Ballistic Capped. These contained about 4.5 lb. of T.N.T. burster and were intended for use against warships of similar class, with a limited number of high-effect rounds with double the explosive content, primarily for shore bombardment. For anti-aircraft protection the ships carried four single 4-in. guns directed by a H.A.C.S.. There were also three quadruple mountings for 0.5-in. machine guns. In 1937, *Ajax* had her heavy A.A. armament doubled with twin Mk XVI twin mountings.

The ships were quite well protected, with a 3-in belt on the sides of the engine and boiler rooms and 1.25-in. deck armour over these spaces. The sides of the magazine were slightly thicker than *Graf Spee*'s belt armour at 3.5-in. with 2-in. horizontal protection. The turrets had 1-in. protection. The scheme was designed to give protection from other light cruisers and destroyers.

The ships were powered by six Admiralty three-drum, water tube boilers feeding four shaft-geared turbines with a total shaft horsepower of 72,000. *Ajax* made just over 33 knots on her trials off Arran in 1935; *Achilles* was slightly slower. The ships were distinctive in having a single trunked streamlined funnel; a single funnel made enemy rangefinding more difficult and its shape and positioning avoided back draughts into the bridge. *Ajax* was fitted as a flagship, which allowed Harwood to use it as a back-up to *Exeter*,

In terms of firepower, *Exeter* could notionally deliver 9,216 lbs of shells per minute, and *Ajax* and *Achilles* 6,400 each, perhaps more. *Achilles*' gunnery officer, Lieutenant R.E. Washbourne, for one, had trained his crews to a loading rate higher than the standard, some nine rounds per minute. This made a total weight of fire for the whole British force of over 22,000 lbs per minute. In return, *Graf Spee* could fire 12,492 lbs of 11-in. shells per minute and, if her shield-protected secondary armament kept up its notionally faster rate of fire of ten rounds per minute, an extra 3,800 lbs of 5.9-in. shells per side. This meant that the *Graf Spee*, far from being at an advantage, was, if it chose to fight at Langsdorff's intended close range, at quite a considerable disadvantage in terms of deliverable firepower, especially considering the vulnerability of its cruiser-standard protection.

Harwood's was in fact a much more powerful force relatively than it has often been portrayed and Langsdorff was putting his head into the lion's mouth engaging it. The initiative was entirely his. The British cruisers had been to dawn action stations but did not fly off the usual dawn air patrol as a later reconnaissance was planned. *Exeter* carried two Walrus amphibians and *Ajax* a single Fairey Seafox, but aircraft flights were rationed as the force only had one fully operational flight, the Seafox. Seaplane operations in the open ocean were very tricky and *Exeter*'s Walruses were not yet fully worked up. *Ajax* had been engaged on secret infra-red photo-reconnaissance missions to search for suspected German U-boat bases on the Brazilian coastline and, contrary to normal practice, had been authorised to accept possible loss or damage to the aircraft to obtain the pictures, As a result, Woodhouse and his pilot, Lt E.G.D. (Drunky) Lewin: 'Worked ourselves up to a degree of efficiency in recovering our aircraft in rough weather which I should not think had ever been approached by any other team.'[17] There were only two Seafoxes available on the station and the other had been damaged to the extent that its serviceability was in great doubt. Thus, continued Harwood, 'for open sea war *Ajax* provided the only fully worked-up air component and she had only one reliable aircraft; so flights for reconnaissance were rationed'.[18]

The lookouts in the British cruisers had still not sighted *Graf Spee* when they saw the puff of smoke her diesels made as they accelerated the German ship to full speed to make her attack. As we have seen,

Langsdorff had already decided to risk all in a close-range encounter, to sink as many of the British ships as possible because of the danger of shadowing. Harwood had his ships in line ahead – *Ajax*, *Achilles*, *Exeter* – on a course of 060 degrees at 14 knots. At about 0604 hrs, Leading Signalman Swanston in the flagship reported the smoke on the port horizon and, as Officer of the Watch, *Ajax*'s seaplane pilot 'Drunky' Lewin informed Captain Woodhouse and the Commodore by voicepipe. Smoke on the horizon was no cause for immediate alarm, and Lewin mistook *Graf Spee*'s superstructure for more smoke so did not immediately realise that the British ships had found their quarry. The cruisers were more than half expecting to meet a British merchantman to take a message into Montevideo so as to be able to maintain radio silence, and Harwood at 0614 hrs flashed a signal to *Exeter* 'Investigate smoke bearing 324 degrees. If this is a British merchant vessel bound for the Plate due to get in harbour soon transfer your signal to her.'[19]

Exeter had also spotted the smoke and signalled by flag at 0615: 'Have sighted smoke bearing 320 degrees.' The heavy cruiser swung to port and at 0616 hrs flashed the electrifying signal: 'I think it is a pocket battleship.' *Exeter*'s torpedo officer, Lt Cdr C.J. Smith, now identified the contact positively as a pocket battleship of the Scheer class and the British heavy cruiser made the flag signal N322, meaning 'enemy in sight, bearing 322.' By this time, prompted by Swanston, Lewin had also changed his mind and sounded the ship's alarm. As the rattlers buzzed the morse letter 'A' and the Royal Marine bugler sounded 'action stations', Harwood slipped the first available uniform over his orange pyjamas and rushed to the bridge. Two minutes later, at 0617 hrs, as the three cruisers unfurled their battle ensigns, *Graf Spee* opened fire. Harwood signalled to *Achilles* by flags at 0622: 'Alter course together to 340 degrees', then, a minute later: 'Open fire G25' (i.e. Open fire, guide of fleet intends to proceed at 25 knots). He also initiated a report of the enemy's course and speed, broadcast to the fleet at 0634 hrs.[20] The hunters had their quarry at bay; the Battle of the River Plate had begun.

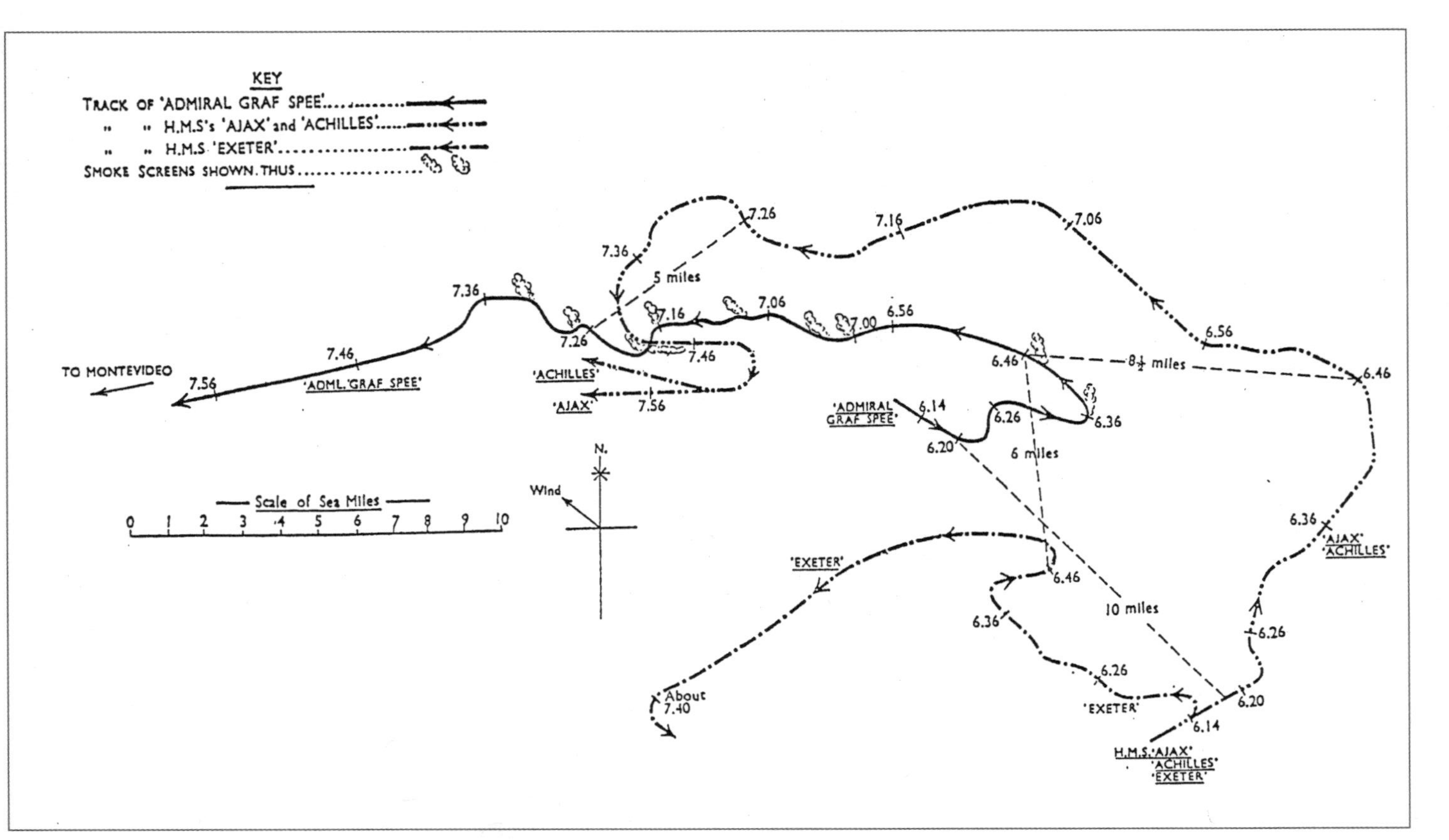

Action between H.M. ships *Ajax*, *Exeter* and *Achilles* and *Admiral Graf Spee*, 13 December 1939.

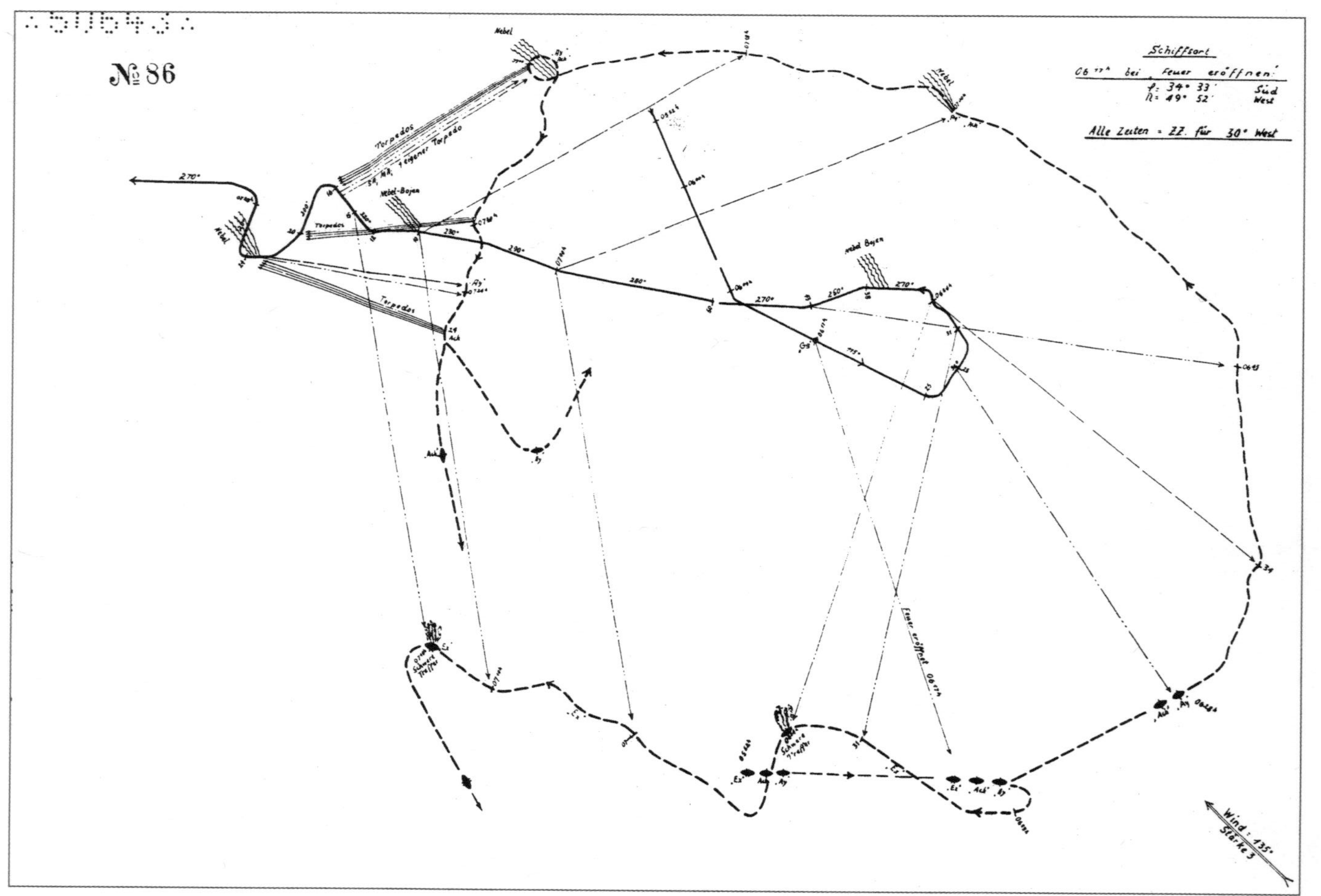

'*Admiral Graf Spee* during the engagement in the South Atlantic against the British Cruisers *Exeter*, *Achilles* and *Ajax* on 13, 12, 1939' – *The German Story*.

CHAPTER FIVE

The Battle[1]

Langsdorff's next decision, after the fatal one of engaging in the first place, was to close the range as rapidly as possible before the British could work up to effective fighting speed. He increased to his maximum speed – which, given the state of *Graf Spee*'s engines, came out at about 24 knots. Langsdorff knew he had to sink or disable all three enemy ships, as shaking off a shadower would be difficult. At 06.05 hrs, *Graf Spee* signalled the warships for identification and ran up a masthead flag. Five minutes later the two smaller ships were identified as Leander class light cruisers, and at 06.12 hrs *Graf Spee* altered course to 115 degrees for a running fight to starboard. The Panzerschiff's fate was now in the hands of her gunnery officers. Korvettenkapitän Ascher fired the main armament from the foretop director, Korvettenkapitän Kurt Meusemann, the third gunnery officer, the 5.9-in. guns and Korvettenkapitän Hans Fuchs, in charge of A.A. armament, the 4.1-in. guns that had a significant anti-surface capability also.

Ascher's first target was *Exeter*, and *Graf Spee* opened fire at 0617 hrs at a range of 19,700 metres. Firing was painfully slow, only four 11-in., three-gun salvos, each from the after turret, in the first five minutes. The vibration of the ship's diesels made the operation of the 11-in. guns difficult. The state of *Graf Spee*'s engines limited her speed close to her critical speed of maximum resonance of 21 knots.[2] As a result, *Graf Spee* was having serious problems with her fore turret, a small screw in the electrical magneto in the machinery aiming off the guns in elevation to the correct fire control solution having shaken loose, perhaps as the ship passed through the critical speed. This seized up the turret, which at first could only fire when the ship turned to starboard to bring it on to the target. The middle gun had to be disconnected to operate independently so that the turret could traverse. Nevertheless, German gunnery lived up to its reputation for early accuracy. Ascher was short with his first 400-yard spread ranging salvo but straddled with the second. One shell of the third salvo landed close by on *Exeter*'s starboard side. Its splinters killed most of the starboard torpedo crew, riddled the starboard of the two Walrus aircraft and pierced the ship's side, killing two men and damaging the ship's gunnery and steering communications.

Ascher had used base-fused, high-effect rounds to find the range for easier spotting but having done so, changed to nose-fused explosive ammunition. He calculated the high-effect shells would be more effective than armour-piercing against what he regarded as the relatively light protection of the British cruiser, and would cause greater splinter damage even with near-misses. The state of the fore turret caused him to continue in salvo firing for a time, giving Harwood the impression that he had succeeded in confusing the fire of the *Graf Spee*'s main armament. At 0620 hrs, *Exeter* returned fire at 18,700 yards using her two forward turrets. *Exeter*'s firing was also slow and deliberate, with one salvo every half minute or so. The cruiser's gunnery officer, Lt Commander Jennings, achieved a straddle with his third shot. He now ordered a zigzag grouping of his guns. He could also now use his after turret, as permission was given to accept damage to the already wrecked aircraft. No sooner were all guns bearing than a hit was scored by the fifth or sixth salvo on the *Graf Spee*'s starboard 4.1-in. A.A. mounting, killing half the crew. The shell penetrated thirty-two feet through two decks and exploded in the searchlight workshop. It knocked out the gun mounting, the starboard chain hoist for 4.1-in ammunition, the searchlight workshop and, most importantly, the fresh water plant. A near-miss also caused damage, bursting just abaft the fore turret, making holes in the anti-torpedo bulge and the ship's side above with splinters.

Graf Spee gave as good as she got, especially when her fore turret was back in operation and she was able to move to six-gun broadsides. A second German 11-in. hit went through the embarkation hatch abaft *Exeter*'s B turret, and passed through the sick bay before exiting the port side. Happily its fuse was not activated. Not so the shell that hit at 0624 hrs on the 1-in. armour protection of 'B'-turret, ahead of the bridge. The round exploded on impact and the turret was put out of action (but not completely wrecked). More seriously, perhaps, the bridge was swept by splinters. All on it were killed, except Captain Bell and the torpedo control and firing officers. Communications from the wheelhouse were wrecked and Bell, wounded in the face, made his way to the after control position. The transmitting gear here was out of action too, probably as a result of the first near-miss. The ship had begun to swing to starboard and the Torpedo Officer, Lt Cdr C.J. Smith, contacted the after steering position to keep the firing arcs open. Bell found Midshipman Bonham in the after control position and sent him down to the after steering position with more helm orders. Within only a few minutes of the serious hit, Bell was successfully conning the ship using a chain of sailors to pass orders down between the after positions.

Exeter had kept speeding west north westerly, firing with her remaining armament. A number of near-misses were obtained but no hits. *Graf Spee* was luckier. She scored two more hits on *Exeter* forward, and near-misses continued to shower the ship with splinters, causing more casualties. *Graf Spee*'s attention was, however beginning to shift to the two British light cruisers which she had been engaging with her starboard 5.9 in guns. One rating in *Achilles* remembered the events of The Glorious 13th as beginning thus:

> Dawn action stations exercised 05.30. We had just turned back in our hammocks for about twenty minutes when suddenly at 06.20

> the alarm rattles sounded off. "Whew! Hell! What the blazes is up now? – Somebody playing a blinkin' joke on us?" These were a few of the exclamations we all said. However, in a matter of seconds we were out on the upper deck. This is what I saw and heard. I was No. 6 on Port 2 High Angle gun. "Whacko! That was a close splash near the stern. The blinkin' *Exeter* is doing a throw-off shoot. Hell! no; it's the bloody *Scheer*! Go on, don't make me laugh – By cripes! You're right, it's her all right!"[3]

Harwood's First Division had continued on their course, 060 degrees. The gun crews closed up as rapidly as possible and both ships opened fire at about 0622 hrs, *Achilles* before *Ajax*. The light cruisers were each firing a broadside once every 15 seconds to find the range as they turned to port at 25 knots to close it. At about 0625 hrs, the two British cruisers were able to achieve concentration of fire using wireless. Effectively the two ships were firing as one, with *Ajax* as the 'master ship', but they were over the target as their plot of *Graf Spee*'s course was innacurate. Down corrections were made, and by 0628 hrs Langsdorff was being straddled with combined broadsides of sixteen shells. By this time, according to the Germans, he had turned to port on the advice of his torpedo officer, who was afraid that the two light cruisers might carry out a torpedo attack from their bearing of 020 to 025 degrees. At this time, with *Exeter* blazing from his hits, Langsdorff ordered his 11-in. guns to shift to *Ajax*. The light cruisers had become a threat, although at this stage they had scored few, if any hits. *Ajax* was straddled three times by 11-in. shells at about 0631 hrs and turned away a little to starboard to throw off the fire. Harwood still thought *Graf Spee* had divided its fire, but Ascher was using his entire main armament once more in three-gun salvos to obtain the range.

Exeter now had a short but welcome respite. She was taking water forward both from action damage and the attempts to put out fires in the forecastle started by the hits. *Exeter*'s torpedo officer, a survivor of the mayhem on the cruiser's bridge, Lt Cdr C.J. Smith, had gone to the starboard tubes and with a scratch crew got them back into action. The range was long for a torpedo engagement, about 13,000 yards, but Lt Cdr Smith thought his Mk VIIs could do it and at 06.31 hrs, under local control, fired three torpedoes set into the area his sights told him *Graf Spee* was sailing. Unfortunately for Smith, the torpedoes missed and were not even spotted by the Germans, who were turning to port. Langsdorff was worried that their current course would lead to Harwood crossing their 'T'. This also allowed *Graf Spee* conveniently to re-engage the heavy cruiser, which had now emerged from the smoke of her wounds. An intensive broadside duel developed between the ships that went on for about ten destructive minutes.

Exeter had only four 8-in. guns remaining but she kept up what was, in the circumstances, a remarkably accurate bombardment of the pocket battleship. She hit the enemy twice. One shot passed through the *Graf Spee*'s tower mast and exploded clear of the ship. The other hit was more serious and shocked the Germans severely. It penetrated the top of *Graf Spee*'s main armour belt below the conning tower and had enough energy also to penetrate the next armoured splinter bulkhead before exploding amidships in a workshop. This hit probably occurred when the Panzerschiff was turning, as the round seemed to have skimmed over the heeling deck before exploding as it hit the armoured deck, bending it into a dish shape about 1-in. deep over an area of about a yard and killing several German ratings. This could have been a very serious hit indeed for the Germans, for if it had been just three feet further aft it would have entered the engine rooms. Panzerschiffe were vulnerable to heavy cruisers after all! As it was, important cabling to the foretop fire control was cut. A third shell near-missed, splinters holed *Graf Spee*'s port side.

It was therefore fortunate for the Germans that they were now able to halve *Exeter*'s reduced armament. As the cruiser was completing a turn to starboard to fire her port torpedo tubes, an 11-in. round struck forward on 'A'-turret, putting it out of action. *Exeter* then fired her remaining torpedoes – to little effect – and was struck twice more. One 11-in. round hit the navigating officer's cabin, passed through the armament office and went through for about twenty yards or so before bursting on the barrel of the foremost 4-in. A.A. gun on the disengaged starboard side. A number of sailors were killed both inside and outside the superstructure, and exploding 4-in. ammunition from the foremost ready-use locker began to shower the ship with splinters and other debris. Then a second shell hit amidships ahead of the armour belt, penetrating the light plating at that point, passing through three more bulkheads, and exploding in the Chief Petty Officers' Flat on the armoured deck above the 4-in. magazine.

Exeter's protection and anti-flash precautions had done their job and the cruiser did not blow up, but damage was severe as the entire ship shook with the force of the blast. Not only was the C.P.O.'s flat devastated, with all but one of the eighteen men there killed, but a fire was soon raging in the lower servery flat, putting the 4-in. AA, aircraft bomb room and 'B'-turret 8-in. magazines in danger. Sergeant George Puddifoot, Royal Marines, in the 8-in. magazine consulted with Engine Room Artificer Frank Bond and they decided to flood it. Personnel inside the switchboard and forward dynamo rooms were trapped. Stoker Patrick O'Brien led a fire party to rescue them. Most important to the fighting capability of the ship, however, was the destruction by splinters of cabling, including that providing power to the Transmitting Station. The T.S. was evacuated, and *Exeter*'s surviving turret was reduced to uncorrected firing under direct local control. Jennings moved aft to the after searchlight platform to do the best he could to direct Exeter's two last 8-in. guns. The hit also disabled the gyro repeaters, and Bell was reduced to steering the ship using the portable compass from a boat. Despite these normally crippling blows, Bell bravely continued the pursuit of *Graf Spee* with the remnant of her main armament, now bearing once more to fire on the starboard beam.

At 06.34 hrs *Ajax* and *Achilles* had turned back to port to close slightly. *Ajax*'s fire control personnel were having some trouble keeping the range of the target. They thought the speed of *Graf Spee* had been estimated wrongly by the rate officer, so this was first increased to 28 knots and then reduced to 26 and finally to a more accurate 24 knots. 'Down ladders' of shells were resorted to, to spot back onto the target and retune the fire control table. In fact, the inclination of the target seems to have been mistaken too, and only at about 0636 hrs were the true movements of *Graf Spee* being fed into the light cruisers' fire control systems. The Germans were zigzagging to avoid fire and this was probably a major factor in the confusion – although it also affected German shooting. The British gunners thought that *Graf Spee* was approaching them at a sharp angle; in fact she was turning away to engage *Exeter*, first on a north westerly course and then making a larger zigzag to port and then to starboard. This was to bring Ascher's starboard secondary armament to bear on *Ajax* and *Achilles*, on which they opened fire. At about 0636 hrs the British noted that *Graf Spee* had indeed turned and the two side's track charts at last came into some kind of correspondence. Harwood hoisted 'G28' to increase speed to 28 knots.

At 0637 hrs the flagship catapulted off Lieutenant Lewin's Fairey Seafox floatplane to spot for the division. This Harwood considered to be: 'a very fine evolution', as Lewin had to avoid the blast of *Ajax*'s four after guns firing on forward bearings.[4] Indeed, the aircraft would probably have been fatally damaged by gun blast if it had not been catapulted off. Unfortunately, at first, confusion was worse compounded. The aircraft's radio was tuned to the longer wave of 250 k/Cs for reconnaissance rather than the much higher frequency of 3800 k/Cs normally used for spotting. The observer, Lt. R.E.N. Kearney, signalled the flag deck that he would continue on the lower frequency to save time. This message was received on the flag deck but not passed on to the wireless office. It took twelve minutes for *Ajax*'s radio operators to realise the error; and thus, for the next few minutes, the two cruisers had to rely on visual spotting from *Ajax*'s control tower – from where Lieutenant Desmond Dreyer, the flagship's gunnery officer, was still controlling the two ships as one. *Graf Spee* now used her smoke generators to shield her from *Ajax* and *Achilles* as she concentrated on *Exeter*, and this prevented keeping a good range plot although some straddles were spotted and hits continued to be scored.

These returned Langsdorff's attention to *Ajax* and *Achilles*, and he took the opportunity of *Exeter*'s clearly serious damage and obscuring smoke to re-engage the light cruisers with his main armament. His main director was probably out of action by this time due to the 8-in. hit, and his best rangefinder and director was the one back aft. He thus was content to use this with his after turret to engage the light cruisers. The angle was far from perfect, but the long baselength rangefinder was a superb instrument even at the lower elevation of the after director. With what was probably the first salvo after changing target *Graf Spee* scored a near-miss on *Achilles*. The 11-in. shell fell just short but burst with some effect. Three ratings on the forward port A.A. gun were cut down and one later died with a splinter through his lungs. Captain Parry was wounded in both legs and Chief Yeoman Martinson had a knee shattered. Lieutenant Dick Washbourne, the gunnery officer in the director control tower trained to port above the bridge, heard: 'a hideous clang and fairly heavy concussion'. Washbourne crouched down in his seat with head wounds streaming blood, shouting orders for the after control position to take over. He then took stock of the situation. As he remembered it to a friend a month later:

> The DCT resembled a slaughterhouse. Six hits had come inside. The right side was a shambles and the left side untouched. Both my Tels (*telegraphists*) were inert blood stained bundles of serge (*they had suffered multiple injuries*). My PIL FT27 (*Position in Line rangefinder*) operator (*Able Seaman Sherley, working as concentration link rangetaker*) had tumbled back through on top of the Spotting Observer with nauseating wounds in the face and thighs. The Spotting Observer himself (*Sergeant Trimble, Royal Marines*) had lost large portions of both buttocks but he, most gallantly, said nothing at the time and stuck it out. My R. to E.D. (*Range to Elevation and Deflection*) unit operator (*Able Seaman Shaw*) had been in the way of a couple of the

> splinters. Unfortunately I didn't notice this last casualty and we continue to fire for some minutes with a dead man resting quietly in a very natural position against his instrument. This threw out our fire for some time which was a pity. When we did spot it, I ordered a young Ordinary Seaman (*Rodgers, trained as back-up R. to E.D. operator*) across from the inclinometer. He couldn't get rid of his predecessor's mutilated body so he calmly seated himself upon this unpleasantness and worked the instrument for the remaining hour of the action. Five out of the ten of us were out, three for keeps, and others took over quietly and did their stuff like absolute veterans, unmoved by the carnage around them.[5]

Washbourne, noticing he had been hit in the shoulder also, calmly made running repairs and got the D.C.T. back in action almost immediately. Damage to the control tower itself was slight, with no damage to electrical connections or to significant instruments. Even with reduced manning – and non-operative training motor and gyro repeater due to splinter damage elsewhere – it was a more capable fire control director than the limited facility aft. It was also lucky that the two cruisers were in concentration firing at the time, which mitigated the effect of the damage. The two cruisers fired no fewer than thirty-two combined broadsides in the six minutes after damage to *Achilles*' D.C.T., sixteen shells every 11–12 seconds. The main effect of the latter damage was to put *Achilles*' fire out to the right for about ten broadsides until Seaman Rodgers took over. Then, at 0646 hrs, as the two ships turned to port at the 30 knots that had been signalled at 0642, the radio connection between *Ajax* and *Achilles* faded and Washbourne was back on his own. Perhaps understandably in the circumstances, the New Zealand-manned cruiser, a New Zealand-starred blue ensign streaming defiantly from its mainmast, did not shoot desperately well at this stage. Washbourne had great difficulty in keeping line and was forced to fire deflection groups using single-step range corrections. His firing was also far short. Not only had *Achilles*' own fire become ineffective but this had also had negative effects on *Ajax*'s gunnery, as Dreyer was still under the impression that the two ships were firing as a concentrated unit and the flagship's gunnery officer was confused by the erratic fall of shot.

This problem rather mitigated the initial impact of the air spotting that began at 0649 hrs, as radio contact was belatedly established. The presence of the aircraft was potentially very useful, as *Graf Spee* was continuing to lay smoke screens; her guns' smoky propellant charges were also adding to the general murk. Unfortunately, Kearney confused *Achilles*' poor shooting with that of *Ajax* and caused Dreyer to shoot over the target for some minutes. Dreyer had no reason to doubt his aerial spotting, which had worked well in peacetime battle practice. His 'overs' were also largely invisible to him in the conditions. He even ignored the evidence of his rangefinders, which were giving values no less than 4,000 yards different from those on the plot in the transmitting station. The range was still long, 16,000 yards, the two ships turning slightly to starboard at 0656 hrs to keep all their guns bearing; they were now speeding through the water at the 31 knots that had been signalled at 0652. Not until 0703 hrs were the aircraft reports disregarded and, as *Graf Spee* twisted and turned, Dreyer decided to withhold fire briefly at 0706 as he realised he was missing the target.

Graf Spee was also having problems and her firing became erratic also. At, or shortly after, 0700 hrs, Langsdorff seems to have decided that the main armament should be shifted back to the opposite beam to engage *Exeter*, which had reappeared from behind the smoke of her fires, still firing from her after turret. The change of target had negative effects on firing; orders became confused, with the two remaining rangefinders ranging on different ships, from which the rest of the fire control system processing data were derived. *Graf Spee*'s shots landed far over *Exeter*. The constant bombardment from the cruisers was also putting the German range takers off their work. Stereoscopic range finding took calm nerves; these were not calm conditions. Then, at about 0710 hrs, *Graf Spee* began to have problems with her fore turret again. Chief Officer Mallinson of the *Streonshalh*, imprisoned directly under the turret, insisted that the centre and right guns did not fire after about 0710 hrs, and that the right-hand gun was also out of action for a while.[6] The combination of the concussion of firing and the vibration of the ship had proved too much.

Exeter was not hit and continued the action with her last gun. Ramming problems were preventing full use being made of the second weapon in the turret. The firing was ineffective as the after turret crew was underestimating the range, but Langsdorff's last bombardment scored no hit either before the battered British cruiser disappeared again behind smoke. At about 0715 hrs he turned his after turret once more back to the light cruisers that he had left to his 5.9-in. and 4.1-in. guns. Although *Exeter*'s bows were down by about three feet and the ship was listing up to ten degrees to starboard, the engines were still able to drive the ship at just over 29 knots. So hard was the *Exeter* being driven, indeed, that the brickwork in her boilers was melting. The high speed also exacerbated the problem of water flooding in through the holes punched by the 11-in. shell splinters in Exeter's side. At 0729 hrs the flooding short-circuited the electricity supply to the turret and Bell had little alternative but to break off the action. The determined Bell considered ramming the pocket battleship; but it was still being heavily engaged by *Ajax* and *Achilles*, so he decided to take a south westerly course to lick his wounds.

The only consolation for the British was that *Graf Spee*'s own fire control problems and reduced armament continued to make her fire ineffective also. Salvos landed both short and over. It was proving difficult to supply the 5.9-in. batteries with ammunition under the torrent of heavy fire; and after the battle, it was discovered that the inclinometer in the starboard secondary armament director had been damaged by a splinter which had disastrous effects on the shooting of that battery.

Harwood decided the range had to be closed and accepted the temporary loss of the fire of his after turrets to turn to port, increasing speed to maximum to close the pocket battleship as quickly as possible: at 0713 hrs Harwood signalled: 'Proceed at utmost speed'.[7]

Four minutes earlier, Dreyer had begun trying again to find the range with exploratory salvos with his forward guns. *Graf Spee*'s avoiding action and use of smoke remained skilful and *Ajax* had considerable difficulty in obtaining a good fire control solution. *Graf Spee* did better when her after turret returned to the attack against the light cruisers. Immediately *Ajax* was straddled three times by 11-in. shells, although the fire of the secondary guns remained ragged, generally falling between the two British cruisers. The German 11-in. fire forced *Ajax* and *Achilles* into zigzags and this in turn also had a negative effect on their firing, making it slower and less effective than it might have been, especially as only eight guns were bearing.

At 0720 hrs Harwood turned slightly to starboard to open up his ships' 'A' arcs once more. Sixteen 6-in. guns delivered enough shells for at least some to find their mark. The Germans described the two cruisers at this time as 'firing furiously'; and *Graf Spee* began to be hit much more frequently. *Ajax* had fire control problems again and *Achilles* began to take over as the main source of damage to the enemy. The British gunners were heartened by the Seafox reporting 'good shot' as the accurate broadsides hit with effect.

Then at 0725 hrs *Graf Spee* hit back. With all 200 of her nose-fused H.E. shells gone and only a handful of base-fused H.E. remaining, *Graf Spee* was now firing armour-piercing rounds from her 11-in. guns. One of these, fired at about 8,700 yards, hit *Ajax* aft. It ploughed through the outer plating, through bulkheads and a deck, then through the working chamber beneath 'X'-turret until the time fuse exploded it in the flag accommodation. Four of the turret's crew were killed and six wounded, and the turret was disabled – but, unlike in the previous war, there was no ammunition explosion. Part of the base of the shell dented the barbette of 'Y'-turret and disabled that one too. At a single blow, *Ajax*'s armament was reduced by half, and soon one of the forward guns failed as well because of a defective hoist.

With the range now down to less than 11,000 yards, *Ajax* had already decided to try a torpedo attack, which led to some tactical confusion. Up until now the cruisers had been fighting under the most general of tactical instructions. All three captains knew what was expected of them and did it to great effect. All Harwood had to do was make flag signals to indicate his intended speed to *Achilles*, which 'followed father' as required. The system generally worked well but it could not co-ordinate a torpedo attack. At about the time she was hit, *Ajax* began to swing to starboard. *Achilles* followed and planned an attack of her own. As she manœuvred to carry it out, *Ajax* sailed right across the New Zealand cruiser's line of fire to deliver her four port Mk IX torpedoes set to 9,000 yards at 21 knots. These porpoised on entry into the water, which may have alerted the Germans to the attack.

Whether or not the Germans spotted the firing, Langsdorff was very jittery of the torpedo threat. His constant alterations of course to avoid possible attacks infuriated his gunnery officers almost as much as did his frequent changes of target. He may already have given the order to turn hard to port on to a south-westerly course to avoid the torpedo threat of the clearly turning cruisers. This had the effect of curtailing a German torpedo firing from *Graf Spee*'s starboard tubes and only one weapon was launched. Luck was certainly not with the German torpedomen as, to close the range – and ruin the Germans' fire control calculations – *Ajax* and *Achilles* now turned to resume a west–south–westerly course to close the range still more. At 0731 hrs the Seafox reported the German torpedo, that was going to pass astern. Harwood decided: 'not to take any chances' but to turn due south and engage the enemy on the starboard side.[8] After the confusion over *Ajax*'s torpedo attack, Harwood now felt he had to be a little more 'hands-on' in tactical instructions and he ordered *Achilles* by wireless to cross *Ajax*'s stern. After the turn to the south and at the close range of 8,000 yards, Washbourne began to make excellent practice with *Achilles*'s full armament against *Graf Spee*, *Ajax* contributing as she could with her three remaining guns.

The British 6-in. shells had not been as effective as they might have been because of the delayed action fuses of their standard C.P.B.C. shells. These were intended to explode after they had entered a lightly armoured target; but in the event, they often went off after they had passed through lightly protected parts of the ship, or after having bounced off heavy armour. Nevertheless, the German ship had suffered severely from the rain of 6-in. projectiles to which it had been subjected. Three struck near the top of the control tower. One hit and carried away the wind baffles on the forward side of the top platform itself before exploding clear of the ship. Langsdorff, exposed and unprotected on the platform, was wounded by splinters in the shoulder and in the arm. He was then knocked unconscious by the concussion of a second shell that exploded just below. Kapitän Walter Kay, the Executive Officer took over the con briefly until Langsdorff came round to resume command. This projectile was probably the one that entered from the starboard side just below the top platform and which partially burst when it hit the ladder giving access to the foretop before the remains went out the other side. The explosion, partial though it was, came up the ladder, killed two sailors and probably concussed Langsdorff. It also killed Oberleutnant Grigat, who had been the first to spot the enemy masts. He had been ordered by the wounded Langsdorff to return to his normal station. Sadly this was the wrong moment to begin to climb down. He lost his legs and later died. Splinters damaged the right prism of the main range finder and the second shell also blew a hole in the deck, and may have cut the cable duct leading up to the main director. The effect of this is uncertain. Post-battle examination concluded that the foremast fire control must have been isolated but the Germans claimed this was not so.[9] The damage to the rangefinder itself was fatal enough (and the 8-in. hit through the belt did cut the cables to the main director for the rest of the action). A third 6-in. entered just below this second hit, went through the tower and exploded over the top of the forward high-angle director, which was not seriously damaged. Rasenack graphically recounted the atmosphere around Langsdorff under fire:

> When our commander received information about the type of units that were opposing us, he said dryly and without taking out his

> pipe from the corner of his mouth: "These we will smash", and instead of going to the armoured command post, he went to the wings of the flying bridge. From there he is better able to see what is happening and direct the action. Even when shrapnel and splinters are flying about, and when everybody automatically takes shelter behind the armour plates he remains standing firmly and quietly giving his orders. He is wounded twice: in the shoulder and in the arm. He bleeds freely. Yet, he only allows an emergency dressing to be put on. At another moment the blast of the explosion of a shell knocks him to the ground and he loses consciousness. The First Officer is called and he continues directing the action but our captain shortly comes to and again takes over command.[10]

One British shell worked very well. It entered the starboard boat deck, passed fifty feet through the ship's company galley and detonated inside on the upper deck, causing considerable damage. Also damaged was the 5.9-in. ammunition hoist to the forward port side. A charge was in the hoist but its protective casing prevented a secondary explosion. The hoist itself was disabled, as was the power supply for the forward magazine group, which moved to emergency supply. Yet another 6-in. shell came over the ship from starboard and devastated number three gun on the port side. Captain Dove, still a prisoner on the pocket battleship, saw it happen:

> One moment there was a gun about to be fired and men working on it. Then there came a blinding flash and an explosion, which sent me reeling back into the flat thinking that I was hit. The bulkhead of the housing just above me was shattered. Bits of debris came flying through the skylight. When, a second later, I climbed up and looked again, the gun's crew had vanished. The gun itself lay drunkenly on one side, its muzzle pointing downwards. The shield was riddled with holes, and the steel door behind the breech had been torn off its hinges. Every man of that gun's crew had been wiped out in that instant. The same shell smashed the jib of the

> electric crane on the port side, and shattered the launch stowed on the skids under it. From where I stood, I could look forward along the port side to the bridge. It was just one huge litter of wreckage. Bits of the ship's rail, twisted pieces of steel, shattered pieces blown from the ship's launches, broken gun rams and other wreckage lay strewn everywhere.[11]

The shell had hit the superstructure just aft of the port side control tower before bursting. All the gun's crew were indeed killed and electrical leads and instruments were destroyed, but the gun itself was undamaged. A practice shell loaded in error by *Achilles* hit on the starboard quarter of *Graf Spee* aft and passed through half a dozen cabins, killing two ratings and cutting cables before coming to rest in the Warrant Officers' quarters in the port half of the ship. A more normal C.P.B.C. entered beneath the bridge through the 37-mm ready-use lockers, which were set on fire. It then detonated at the base of the high- angle control tower, cutting the cables to the gyro stabilising. Another entered the Admiral's cabin under the after rangefinder, detonating and ruining the cabin but causing no serious structural or fire control damage. Another went through the fore part of the lower bridge/night control position without detonating inside the ship; nevertheless, damage was inflicted on the cabling of the port torpedo training mechanism and the searchlights. Two other hits from starboard damaged the officers' boats on each side.

At least three 6-in. shells bounced off the main armour of the turrets, one forward and two aft, one of the latter exploding after bouncing clear. Serious structural damage was, however, caused by a hit on the starboard bow which burst on the port side skin, blowing a large hole of two square yards on the port side of the low forecastle, causing serious flooding of the forward mess deck and significantly compromising the seaworthiness of the ship. Another hit further forward also damaged the port side of the forecastle, starting a fire in the damage control material storeroom. At least fourteen 6-in. hits on *Graf Spee*'s hull and upperworks were scored from starboard, with other near-misses, and the British ships could see that they had at least caused some, if limited, damage.[12] An ammunition fire burned on deck unattended, the remains of the Arado seaplane were gutted by fire. Splinters from hits and near-misses destroyed the catapult turning gear and damaged the optical equipment in the conning tower, the starboard forward 37-mm guns, two searchlights and the right barrel of the port 4.1-in. A.A. mount. There were four small leaks in the port side and two in the starboard, which the damage control parties successfully blocked off.

Langsdorff and his crew were shaken. They thought they saw two further torpedo attacks and made starboard turns accordingly, coming round to the west, before turning to the north-east under cover of smoke; and then finally, at about 0730 hrs, turning westwards on course 270 degrees. *Graf Spee* could still bite back, however as Lewin found when he tried to close in his Seafox to inspect damage. He was engaged by A.A. fire and a wing was holed. The floatplane then took up position on *Ajax*'s disengaged side. At 0736 hrs, *Graf Spee* re-engaged *Ajax* and *Achilles* on the port side. Both ships claimed hits, but the Germans only recorded one 6-in. hit on the hull of the ship from port. It hit the cutter on that side of the ship before detonating in the ventilation hatch to number three engine room. This was quite a serious hit which damaged the chain hoist to the port 5.9-in. armament and inflicted heavy splinter damage on the auxiliary boiler stack. The speed of the ship dropped for a short time but then recovered. However, another port side 6-in. hit which does not appear in German accounts of the battle damage was a round that was later clearly seen in Montevideo sticking unexploded out of the top of *Graf Spee*'s belt, about three feet above the water line. Coincidentally, it had hit close to *Exeter*'s penetrating hit, above and to the right. The shell did not burst but remained there with about six inches protruding. *Graf Spee*'s armour belt could defeat the lighter shells and British observers noted evidence of up to half a dozen more hits on the *Graf Spee*'s side further aft that had not penetrated at all.[13] The three hits the Germans noted bouncing off the turrets were also all on the port side, though some at least could have occurred from starboard when the after turret was traversed.

Graf Spee's main armament also regained some of its initial accuracy under the control of the after control position. One 11-in. shell from the aft turret cut *Ajax*'s main topmast in two. It was not seen to explode, but splinters from overhead inflicted casualties on the personnel on the after superstructure. These could have come from *Graf Spee*'s after 4.1-in. mounting that was firing time-fused shell at *Ajax*. The Commodore now received a message that the flagship was down to only 20 per cent of his 6-in. ammunition. This was a mistake, as the report referred only to 'A'-turret that had been heaviest engaged; but the news caused Harwood to retire until after dark, when he thought he would try a night action, something for which the Royal Navy had been training hard throughout the 1930s, and in which it believed it had an advantage. So, at 0740 hrs, after some eighty minutes of intensive action, *Ajax* and *Achilles* altered course to the east and retired under cover of smoke. Much to the relief of those in the cruisers, Langsdorff made no move to follow. Instead he took *Graf Spee* at 22 knots westward into the Plate estuary. After six minutes, Harwood ordered his two operational cruisers to turn to shadow the enemy, one cruiser on each quarter. Langsdorff's confident gamble had gone terribly wrong. He had not overwhelmed his opponents. Instead, far from home and with damage that his crew considered 'terrific', he was being chased towards neutral waters by enemy ships that could evade his fire and call up fatally superior forces. The prospects were bleak.

CHAPTER SIX

Pursuit[1]

Harwood had little trouble maintaining contact with *Graf Spee*, whose control tower made a conspicuous point of attention fifteen miles away. At 0807 hrs the Commodore, temporarily out of wireless touch because of the loss of *Ajax*'s mast, ordered *Achilles* to inform all British merchant ships of the pocket battleship's position course and speed. With jury-rigged aerials, *Ajax* was also soon back on the air and every hour made similar situation reports.

Exeter was also out of communication because of aerial damage and Harwood sent Lewin and his Seafox to find her and order her to rejoin. As the floatplane found and closed the heavy cruiser it was clear she was in a very poor state. Kearney, the observer, reported that: 'She was obviously hard hit and in no condition to fight another action', while Lewin remarked that he had: 'Never seen such a shambles, anyway in a ship which survived.'[2] At 0912 hrs, *Ajax* recovered her Seafox and again began shadowing. Harwood was in need of reinforcement and at 0946 hrs made to *Cumberland* to cut short her refit and make best speed to the Plate.

Harwood had placed *Cumberland* at eight hours' notice for steam, but her engineering officer thought that too long and arranged for her self-refit to be managed by units, with two of the four shafts ready for use at only two hours' notice. These could give 25 knots while the other two shafts were put back into action. *Cumberland* picked up her group's action messages, and Fallowfield immediately made ready for sea. The first signal for him to sail arrived in garbled form at 0946 but he assumed its meaning and sailed at 1000 hrs. He had already sailed by the time Harwood's message arrived as a routine repetition, just at the moment his two extra shafts came back on line. Speed was duly increased to 30 knots and held at that for thirty-four hours.

Shortly after 1000 hrs, *Achilles* drifted too close to *Graf Spee*, which turned to fire the right hand gun of the fore turret twice at the New Zealand cruiser. Langsdorff's use of the fore turret alone at this stage was probably because the after turret that had fired more rounds in action had less ammunition remaining. The first shot was short but the second was much closer. *Achilles* opened the range under cover of smoke. Washbourne, her gunnery officer, was far from confident, as he wrote to a friend later: 'Now we refer to this phase of the operation proudly and confidently as The Chase, that was not our attitude at the time. It was unimaginable that this fine ship, with at least one 11-in. turret and one 5.9-in. in action, and almost her full speed, should be belting from one and a half small 6-in cruisers both almost out of ammunition. We thought that she must have something up her sleeve, and we watched eagerly for the next development.'[3]

Achilles' ratings were feeling rather better, especially after their daily tots of rum. 'and did we need them? 12.25. Very nerve wracking and much excitement during the rest of Thursday; but everyone quite calm and cool. Yeah! After our rum!'[4]

Things did not seem that favourable on board *Graf Spee*. She had been hit at least twenty-three times, probably three times by *Exeter* and about twenty by *Ajax* and *Achilles.* One officer and 36 ratings had been killed and 57 more wounded. Although *Graf Spee* was basically seaworthy and still capable of fighting, her damage was greater than immediately apparent and she had lost some vital equipment that reduced significantly both her combat capability and her ability to make oceanic voyages. The main galley and bakery facilities on the

The vanquished: Kapitän-sur-Zee Hans Wilhelm Langsdorff

The victor: Admiral Sir Henry 'Bobby' Harwood

'Our Man in Montevideo' – Sir Eugen Millington-Drake

Millington-Drake greets Admiral Harwood on the occasion of his triumphal visit to Montevideo in *Ajax*. On the left is Lewin. (*Jill Quaife*)

Presenting the Willingdon medals. On the left of the picture is Harwood, on the right McCall. The diplomatic offensive did much to ensure the alignment of 'neutral' South America with the Allied cause. (*Jill Quaife*)

Graf Spee's foremast tower bears the 'Coronel' battle plate. Note the heightened director tower with the long baselength optical rangefinder and the mounting for the radar antenna; with, bottom left, the forward high-angle director and twin 37mm A.A. mounting. (*Author*)

A fine pre-war view of HMS *Exeter* on the South American station. (*Harwood Collection*)

Exeter turns and engages to starboard. She would have looked much like this in the battle. (*Lumley Collection*)

Crowds line the quayside in Montevideo as *Graf Spee* sails into the dusk. (*Jill Quaife*)

HMS *Ajax* visiting Montevideo after the battle, still in the state in which she fought the action. Prominent on the catapult is Lewin's Seafox. (*Jill Quaife*)

Exeter's holed funnels. Shrapnel from near-misses proved almost as devastating as actual hits. (*Lumley Collection*)

Exeter's battered 8-in. fore turrets. (*Lumley Collection*)

A slightly blurred forward view of *Graf Spee* in Montevideo harbour, clearly showing the large hole in the bow that must have cast doubt on her seaworthiness. Note also the drooping middle gun in the forward 11-in. turret. It has been disconnected to allow the turret to train. (*Lumley Collection*)

The damaged Panzerschiff in Montevideo. The after 11-in. turret and long-base rangefinder that bore the brunt of the latter part of the action are clearly visible. (*Lumley Collection*)

Graf Spee's dead come ashore. Swastika flags give the lie to subsequent propaganda regarding the symbolism of Langsdorff shooting himself on the battle ensign. (*Jill Quaife*)

The cost of war: burying *Graf Spee*'s dead. Langsdorff (in uniform) and the German ambassador, Langmann, are pictured together, *centre*. (*Jill Quaife*)

Scuttled. Explosions wrack *Graf Spee*. (*Imperial War Museum*)

Graf Spee burns as a tugboat looks on. The leaning funnel is clearly visible. (*Lumley Collection*)

The burned-out hulk rests on the shallow mud. Now the wrangling begins over the wreck. (*Jill Quaife*)

What Vega purchased with the Admiralty's money . . . The vital radar is still clearly visible, as the wreck settles deeper in the mud. (*Lumley Collection*)

Triumphal return of HMS *Exeter* to Devonport, England, February 1940. Her turrets had been repaired with corrugated iron sheets obtained from Falkland Islanders' sheds. (*Lumley Collection*)

upper deck had been put out of action and the flour store was contaminated with seawater. The key auxiliary boiler that supplied steam to the distilling plant for fresh water and the fuel and lubricating oil purifier was also out of action. The large hole in the bows also seriously compromised the ship's capacity to take the heavy seas of the North Atlantic if she was to return home. These factors weighed heavily on Langsdorff's mind as he made his rounds of the ship to see the damage for himself.

There was significant damage to the ship's armament that could not be repaired by the crew. The forward A.A. director was out of action because of a hit in its base. The starboard 4.1-in. gun mounting and the right barrel of the port mounting were disabled, as was the starboard chain hoist for 4.1-in. shells. All this made the ship much more vulnerable to air attack and, perhaps more importantly, to air reconnaissance and spotting. The port ammunition hoists for the 5.9-in. guns had been disabled, slowing down the rate of fire of the guns on that side of the ship. The port torpedo training mechanism was destroyed, as were one of the tubes and other important parts of the torpedo fire control equipment and the starboard torpedo spread apparatus. *Graf Spee* had effectively lost her torpedo armament – a point of some salience to a torpedo officer like Langsdorff. The forward 11-in. gun turret's reliability was doubtful. Most important of all, however, was the fact that, even if the cabling to it could be repaired, the ship's main rangefinder, in the foretop director, had been disabled by fragments. *Graf Spee*'s main means for finding and ranging on targets was out of action.

This was another decisive moment. Langsdorff weighed the options as carefully as his wounds allowed. It must have been hard for the Captain to be totally rational. Several of his subordinates remarked how he seemed affected by his wounds and became more erratic and less considered. This had had effects on the latter part of the action. Now it affected his judgment after it. The first-aid posts were running with the blood of his mangled personnel and this must have affected his stress level. His decision alone had led to their wounds.

Langsdorff's sense of duty to his men also made him conscious of their need for fully functioning food and water provision. Most importantly, the vital fuel and oil purification plant was perhaps irreparable at sea, as were significant parts of his fighting capacity. Not far away were a number of ports where he could lick his wounds and reassess his options. The aggressiveness and 'courageous decision' of the British cruisers also seemed to indicate the presence of heavier forces out to sea.[5]

According to his remarks to Captain Dove the following day, this last point was an especially important factor. He said that the cruisers would never have acted as they did unless they were supported by big ships. 'My intelligence tells me that the *Barham* and *Dunkerque* were in the vicinity. The British cruisers tried to cut me off from the shore and drive me out to sea. They would never have dared do this unless they had some support or were trying to drive me out into the guns of bigger ships somewhere out to sea'.[6] The choice thus seemed to Langsdorff to be between the near-certainty of interception by heavier units in his present state – he did not give much for his chances of seeing off his shadowers – or taking his chance of a break-out in a more seaworthy and fully operational vessel.

A cooler and less pain-wracked judgement might have considered the near-certainty that the proximate enemy heavy units would assemble off any port in which he entered, and that it might well thus, effectively, become a trap. This was the view of his subordinates when, at the conclusion of his tour of the ship, Langsdorff announced his plans to enter a River Plate port. Such was their respect for their charismatic commander, however, that they neither argued with the basic idea nor put the case for the potentially friendlier Argentine ports, Rio Grande da Sol or Puerto Belgrano. Reaching both the latter required a longer period of night-time vulnerability to his pursuers' torpedoes. The politically aware Langsdorff does not seem to have been briefed on the pro-British feelings in Montevideo and the difficulties they might create for him. Lines of communication between the German Navy and Foreign Office were not strong in the bureaucratically fissured Third Reich. Langsdorff settled on Montevideo as the easiest available refuge. He signalled his intentions in his report of the engagement to Raeder.

At 1100 hrs, a merchant ship was sighted by *Graf Spee* coming in the opposite direction. She was identified as the British steamer *Shakespeare*, which eventually stopped and blew off steam after a 5.9-in. shell was fired across her bows. Langsdorff, rather cheekily, signalled to *Ajax* on her pre-war call sign to prepare to pick up her boats. This was the first proper identification of their quarry the British had received; up to then they thought they had been fighting *Admiral Scheer*. In the circumstances, neither *Graf Spee* nor Harwood had any intention of stopping nor, in the circumstances, did *Shakespeare* bother to lower her boats. The relieved master of the *Shakespeare* signalled to Harwood that he had no need of assistance and she was soon back under way. The Germans had decided that it would be politically unwise to sink a merchantman, even one that disobeyed their orders, just before entering a neutral port.

At this time, Harwood received a signal via *Exeter*'s jury-rigged aerials on her condition. The ship had been righted by pumping fuel but she was three feet down by the bows and capable of only eighteen knots. His brave former ship was clearly of no further fighting value, and Harwood ordered her to make for the Falklands for repairs. As the pursuit closed the Plate estuary, Harwood at 1347 hrs signalled Captain H. McCall, the Naval Attaché at Buenos Aires, to arrange for the entrances to the river to be watched; this was duly done with local tugs and aircraft.

Twice in the afternoon, at about 1400 and 1500 hrs, *Graf Spee* turned to fire her forward 11-in. gun at *Achilles*, but these shots made little impression and were not even mentioned in British reports. At about 1530 hrs, Washbourne in *Achilles* had what he later reported as his real worst moment of the day: 'Away on the starboard bow we sighted a ship bearing down on our procession... Then to our horror other unwanted details came up, each of which in turn made more certain that it was a Hipper. I had only a few days previously drawn her silhouette myself. When there was no doubt I told the captain. The bridge agreed, sadly.'[7]

At 1543 hrs, *Achilles* signalled 'enemy in sight, 297' and later amplified this to a 'suspected 8-in. cruiser.' Soon however it was clear that it had been a false alarm and the 'Hipper' turned out to be the modern Lamport and Holt steamer *Delaine*, whose streamlined funnel had caused the confusion. At 1559 hrs the enemy sighting report was negatived – to much relief in *Achilles* and *Ajax.*

During the afternoon the Germans continued to carry out repairs to *Graf Spee*. The secondary armament, except for port number three mounting was returned to service (albeit with ad hoc ammunition arrangements) in the expectation of a possible night action. Langsdorff had received Raeder's approval of his intention to enter Montevideo, and at about 1800 hrs the coast of Uruguay came into sight. Just over an hour later, Harwood ordered *Achilles* to follow the pocket battleship if she went west of Lobos and to take advantage of territorial waters to shadow in comparative safety. Indeed, a few minutes later at 1915 hrs *Graf Spee* decided to have another snarl at her pursuers as *Ajax* came within range, and turned to fire two 11-in. salvos. with all four of her available guns. The first fell short, while the second fell in the wake of the turning cruiser, which retreated under cover of smoke. The Germans thought they saw a torpedo track from a submarine and continued to zigzag to protect themselves from this imagined threat. Then an apparent new menace appeared ahead in the shape of a surface warship. Alarms were sounded, but the vessel turned out to be the Uruguayan gunboat *Uruguay*, which had sailed from Maldonado to investigate the activities of the foreign warships in the waters over which the local state claimed jurisdiction. She passed close astern of *Graf Spee* before moving over to inspect the British cruisers. From the supposed safety of Uruguayan waters, the passengers of the French liner *Formose*, bound for Montevideo, observed events with much interest and not a little trepidation, as it was uncertain against whom *Graf Spee* was firing. Preparations were made to abandon ship, but *Graf Spee*'s days as a mercantile raider had ended.

****

As *Ajax* proceeded south of the English Bank to guard against *Graf Spee* doubling back, Captain Parry took *Achilles* to the north of Lobos Island. At sunset the pocket battleship was silhouetted against the afterglow, and *Achilles* was virtually invisible in the darkness against the land. *Graf Spee*'s radar was turned aft to try to help keep in touch with her pursuers in the gathering gloom; but it was of little or no use at such ranges, that still remained above 30 km, twice the range of the set. *Achilles* was outside the three-mile limit recognised by the British Empire but within the waters claimed by both Argentina and Chile. This did not stop another exchange of fire at 2055 hrs. The exact circumstances were the subject of some controversy at the time, as both ships were by now inside the territorial waters claimed by Uruguay. The balance of evidence is that *Achilles* could not resist the tempting target of the pocket battleship, clearly silhouetted against the skyline.[8] She may have been provoked by *Graf Spee* apparently training her turrets, but she certainly fired five broadsides at 22,000 yards, two of which straddled the target. *Graf Spee* replied with three salvos from her after turret, which near-missed the cruiser. Her gunners surprised the British by their accuracy, considering *Achilles* was hard to find against the darkness of the land. Neither side scored any hits and *Achilles* turned away, making smoke. The after range finder was probably ranging on the *Achilles*' flashes; at this range, the radar could not provide even a clue. The Germans might also have been helped by the lights of cars ashore. At about 2140 hrs, *Graf Spee* fired at least two more salvoes at *Achilles.* Both fell short, and Washbourne, in his official report, wrote that these 'Parthian shots were more in the nature of a gesture than effective action'.[9]

Montevideo came clearly into sight as *Graf Spee* moved towards the city, reducing speed to eighteen knots in the shallows that had been threatening to clog her cooling water intakes with mud since passing Lobos Island. The shallower draught *Achilles* closed in the murk to within 10,000 yards of her quarry, moving over to *Graf Spee*'s port quarter to silhouette her shape against the lights of Montevideo. At 2317 hrs, in accordance with orders, *Achilles* withdrew to the eastward, establishing a patrol between Flores Island and English Bank. *Ajax* covered the more southerly passage. At 2350 (an hour earlier local summer time) *Graf Spee* entered Montevideo, passing the breakwater to anchor in the anteport. She took no pilot but one of her ex-mercantile officers had sufficient knowledge of the harbour to bring the ship in safely.

Soon two Uruguayan officers, Commander José R. Varela and Engineer Lieutenant Fontana and port officials were clambering up a ladder lowered by the Germans aft. The visitors were somewhat shocked by the conditions they found on board, with *Graf Spee*'s ship's company in a state of exhaustion, hunger, confusion and, apparently, low morale. The Uruguayans were led along a passage, past the ship's surgeon operating on a wounded man, lit only by Christmas tree decorations. They found their way barred by action damage and were taken to Langsdorff's cabin by another route. This may have been a show put on to impress the Uruguayans with the need for an extensive stay for repairs, but it may also have reflected the true nature of conditions aboard the damaged ship.

Langsdorff appeared with a bloodstained head and face, a young medical orderly putting a new bandage on his arm. He was asked to explain his unconventional arrival with neither pilot nor navigation lights, and answered that it was because he had been taken under fire within Uruguayan waters. The Uruguayans offered to treat the German wounded in their hospitals, which had made preparations (this was an offer that had already been made to both sides via the Uruguayan gunboat *Huracan*); but Langsdorff refused a general transfer. Only the most seriously wounded were sent ashore, the first a gunnery rating in danger of losing his sight, followed at 0130 hrs the following morning by the five other most heavily injured personnel.

Others would leave *Graf Spee* soon. Shortly after she dropped anchor, Oberleutnant Herzberg opened the door on the pocket battleship's prisoners (all of whom had escaped the day's battle unscathed). He put it succinctly, in the time-honoured cliché: 'Gentlemen, for you the war is over. We are now anchored in Montevideo harbour, and the Captain has told me to say that you will be freed tomorrow.' [10]

He did not know it, but the war was over for *Graf Spee* also.

CHAPTER SEVEN

Diplomacy and Deception

Britain's man in Montevideo was Eugen Millington-Drake, a member of the victorious Oxford boat race crew in 1911 and long-standing South American specialist.[1] He had first been posted to the area as legation secretary in Buenos Aires at the beginning of 1915 and had been in Uruguay as British Minister since 1934. Millington-Drake was without doubt one of the most popular members of the Uruguayan capital's diplomatic corps. He made a number of goodwill tours over the country and attended sporting events and similar activities. The nation was led in 1939 by General Alfredo Baldomir, who had won the Presidential elections the previous year. The Foreign minister was Dr Alberto Guani, a well-known figure on the international scene, who had been his country's representative in Brussels, Paris and London and who had played a prominent part in the League of Nations. Millington-Drake and Guani were very old friends, having first met at the end of 1914 on the ship taking Guani home from German-occupied Brussels, and Millington-Drake to his appointment in Buenos Aires. They became, as the latter put it, like 'diplomatic uncle and nephew'.[2] This was of considerable assistance to the British. Millington-Drake's relations were also good with General Alfredo Campos, the Minister of Defence.

Uruguay had strong economic connections with Britain, with British control of many companies, including the public utilities. The Germans had been trying to use this as an excuse for anti-British propaganda, and there was a well-organised subversive movement run by the 'Press Officer' of the German legation. To counter this, in 1938 Millington-Drake arranged for medals to be struck for presentation by a visiting British dignitary to long-service employees of British companies, without distinction of rank. This was a great propaganda success – as was Millington-Drake's follow-up tour to present the same medals in the provinces. The scheme was widened to include pensioners, and Millington-Drake presided at another ceremony at the headquarters of the Central Uruguay Railway. The success of these Willingdon medals led to an invitation to Field Marshal Lord Milne (former Chief of the Imperial General Staff) to present medals bearing his name to servicemen at the end of a tour of the country's armed forces and their establishments. This ensured that a very positive relationship was established between Milne and Defence Minister Campos. In fact, Langsdorff could hardly have chosen a less welcoming environment in the whole of Latin America. The country was democratic in nature and genuinely pro-Allied in sympathy. When a German diplomat asked the largest of the three local ship repair yards, Reguschi and Voulminot, to state their terms to repair *Graf Spee* immediately, he got a curt refusal from the managing director, whose father had been the French co-founder of the company and who had lost relatives to the Germans in the First World War. When asked if his refusal was a result of his ancestry he said that in part it was, but it was also because he was a Uruguayan.

Assistance was needed with welding to repair the battle damage and attempts were begun to recruit assistance instead from Argentina. The only ready labour available was provided by the two German ships in harbour, the German-owned Ribereña Del Plata Coal Company (eventually hired as *Graf Spee*'s contractor), and those German volunteer technicians who could be found among other local firms. About eleven skilled workmen, together with an engine and materials provided by the firms of Cippola and Siemens in Buenos Aires, were brought in on the night boat. Langsdorff felt he needed as much time as he could get in Montevideo to carry out necessary repairs. In fact, time was on the Allies' side, as it would allow a concentration of forces that would seal *Graf Spee*'s fate. The Germans indeed soon thought that that concentration was occurring. Keeping watch from the foretop, and without the aid of his telescopic range finder, the gunnery-officer Ascher thought he identified HMS *Renown*, *Graf Spee*'s greatest potential enemy, already off the port. It is common for psychological pressures to induce such illusory 'sightings'.

The beginnings of the diplomatic battle were therefore somewhat paradoxical. The Germans felt they needed more time; but they would in fact have been better served by an early break-out, before heavier Allied forces arrived for real. The British diplomats were angling for the ship to be forced to sail early, although its destruction by Harwood's limited and damaged force was far less assured then than it would have been later, when heavy reinforcements arrived. The reason for these apparently contradictory positions, flying in the face of the evidence, was in part the initial, inaccurate assessment of the position by the British Naval and Intelligence personnel in Montevideo.

The Naval Attaché in Buenos Aires, Captain Henry McCall, had flown over early on the 14th to join the Montevideo-based Staff Officer (Intelligence), Lt Cdr H.D. Johnston.[3] Also in Montevideo was Captain Rex Miller, a former Army officer accredited as an attaché to the legation, but who was in reality MI6 – head of the important Montevideo station, that co-ordinated covert activities over all of South America. Miller's office overlooked the harbour, and McCall took up residence there. McCall and Miller obtained a boat and circled the *Graf Spee* at close quarters. Neither being a naval architect, they concluded that the ship had suffered little damage to compromise her seaworthiness, and that only damage to the fire control system and/or shortage of ammunition could have caused her to flee to the Uruguayan capital. Hence she should be forced to sail as soon as possible to meet her fate at the hands of Harwood's cruisers.

The ambassador was thus informed before he made his initial dèmarche to Guani on the morning of the 14th. He quoted the Hague Convention of 1907, which limited the stay of a belligerent warship in a neutral port to twenty-four hours unless damage impaired its seaworthiness. Such damage could be repaired; but the neutral defined what was the minimum necessary – repairs to improve the ship's fighting force were not allowed – and the work was to be carried out with the least possible delay. He also quoted Article 9 of the Havana Convention that had extended the Hague provisions to ban any repairs to battle damage. The British Minister argued that *Graf Spee*'s stay ought to be limited to twenty four hours, and that if she stayed longer, she ought to be interned. Millington-Drake knew he was pressing his luck somewhat, despite his friendship with Guani. Uruguay abided by the narrower 'Russian' interpretation of the Hague Convention and did not recognise the Havana provisions. Any repairs necessary to assure the armoured ship's seaworthiness were likely to be allowed.

At noon on the 14th, Millington-Drake, together with the French Ambassador, saw Guani again and backed up his note with the argument that the fact she had sailed three hundred miles the previous day meant that *Graf Spee* was by definition seaworthy.[4] Guani was non-committal. He seems to have been genuinely concerned to maintain as even-handed a neutrality as possible. He maintained almost constant contact with the diplomatic representatives of Argentina, Brazil and Chile, as well as those of the USA. He was also in touch with Dr Cantilo, the Foreign Minister of Panama, which hosted the Pan-American Conference that had declared the area off the Americas a neutral zone a month after the war had begun.

Guani had to take refuge in Pan-American solidarity to stand up to undue browbeating from the belligerents. He was already under pressure from the Germans, who were deciding on quite how long a stay they should request. The Naval Attaché from Buenos Aires, Kapitän Dietrich Niebuhr, flew over with two German civilian constructors to assess damage (the British thought the trio were Argentine officers). Together with *Graf Spee*'s Engineering Officer, Korvettenkapitän Klepp, they did an inspection to see how long it would take to make the ship ready for sea. Holes would have to be welded shut and the galley needed a great deal of work. The team assessed the task at two weeks, and Langsdorff asked the German ambassador, Dr Otto Langmann, to ask the Uruguayan authorities for leave to stay for this period.

Langmann had been Minister in Montevideo since the beginning of 1938. His background was as a protestant minister, and he had become fluent in Spanish as a result of pastoral work to German communities in Latin America. He had converted to Nazism in 1933 and rose in the diplomatic service as a party propagandist. Despite everything, Langmann seems to have been quite a pleasant personality, indeed Millington-Drake found his German opposite number quite an agreeable colleague and rival. He felt Langmann had a better 'feel' for the situation than Langsdorff. Certainly, relations between the two Germans were not good. At their first meeting, Langmann had expressed some displeasure at *Graf Spee*'s arrival in such a state and muttered that German honour and prestige only permitted a short stay, like a British ship. The Uruguayans had indeed granted such a stay, of forty-eight hours, in recognition of the amount of time *Graf Spee* had been at sea under wartime conditions. The enemy, he thought, should not be told how effective their cruisers had been. When he visited Guani, however, together with Niebuhr he reluctantly made the bid for fourteen days. Guani took refuge in a Technical Commission formed of Varela and Fontana, who came back on board *Graf Spee* for an independent assessment of the time needed for minimum repairs. The gunboat *Lavalleja* was also made guardship of *Graf Spee* to prevent any unauthorised transfer of men or material without the approval of the Port authorities.

The Commission arrived at 1900 hrs, was met by Langsdorff, Langmann and Niebuhr and given a list of the most serious damage that affected the ship's seaworthiness:

- nine holes on the outer plating, the most important of which were two in the bows, one of about four square metres and the other about half a square metre, with another hole on the starboard waterline;

- fire fighting equipment at reduced efficiency;
- cracks in the stern;
- 'indispensable installations' in galley, bakery and laundry out of action;
- the auxiliary boiler for drinking water needed repairs.

After their inspection, Varela and Fontana reported that there were more holes in the ship than the Germans had claimed, fifteen on the starboard side and twelve on the port; they had not however observed cracks in the stern. The fire fighting problems they did not feel affected seaworthiness. As for the galley, a shell had indeed destroyed one of he cauldrons, its piping and electrical equipment. Repairs were also necessary to the vital auxiliary boiler; but nothing was seen that could not be repaired 'in a provisional manner' in three days. The

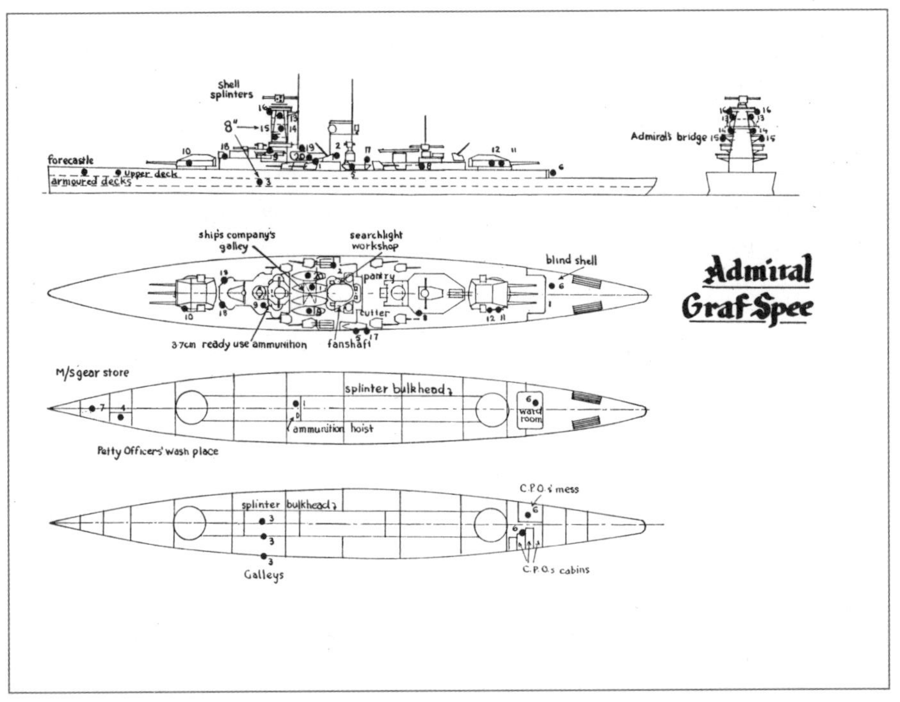

Diagram showing hits to *Graf Spee* (from *The German Story*). Only three are 8-in. shell fire.

following day, therefore, a Presidential Decree was signed giving *Graf Spee* until 2000 hrs on Sunday 17 December to carry out essential repairs.

Early on the morning of Friday 15 December, Millington-Drake received something of a bombshell from Harwood, a request to do everything in his power to delay the pocket battleship's sailing so that reinforcements could arrive. *Cumberland* had been due at 2200 hrs on the 14th, but it would take much longer for decisive reinforcements to arrive. These were the carrier *Ark Royal*, the real battlecruiser *Renown*, the light cruiser *Neptune* (a sister of *Ajax*), the heavy cruisers *Dorsetshire* and *Shropshire* (sisters of *Cumberland*) and three destroyers. The first was not due for five days. A telegram from the Foreign Office backed up Harwood. A shorter time limit, it said, should only be invoked to press the internment case. Otherwise Millington-Drake was to be guided by Harwood.[5]

This vital signal from Harwood had been delayed by the route it had taken via the Falklands and the Cerrito Radio Station. Harwood advised sailing British merchant ships so as to invoke the Hague Convention's twenty-four hour rule that no belligerent warship should leave a neutral harbour until that amount of time had elapsed from the sailing of an enemy merchantman. Harwood also asked Montevideo to keep him informed by regular two-hourly situation reports via Cerrito and the Falklands.

An impressive organisation was built up by the British over the next few days to report on *Graf Spee*. Captain H. Daniel, a former Naval officer and an agent for the Houlder Line, assembled a team of sixteen British pensioners from the local companies and stationed them on board the British merchant ships in Montevideo harbour on a twenty-four hour watch. One ship with observers was berthed right between the *Graf Spee* and the German *Tacoma*. Tugs and motor boats were hired for harbour service and a yacht fitted with a radio was sent out from Buenos Aires to act as a picket in the Plate in case *Graf Spee* took a circuitous route. Harwood could depend on these men to give him *Graf Spee*'s time of sailing and initial course.

Direct communications between Montevideo and belligerent warships was banned but this had not prevented communications corners being cut on local initiative. Shortly after the outbreak of war, Marconi's representative in Montevideo, John Garland, had suggested that the speed and reliability of naval communications in the area could be much improved if a receiving post was set up in the city which could pick up signals from ships for onward delivery through the local Cerrito Radio station to London or the Falkland Islands. Arrangements could also be made for ships to monitor Cerrito Radio at specific times to pick up the signals direct. There was no official money available, but Millington-Drake provided a set, a Skyrider 23, from his own pocket and a Uruguayan telegraphist was employed to help the redoubtable Garland. The listening station was established in the new British Consulate building. The station picked up and forwarded to London *Achilles*'s signal that the battle had begun, the first information available that the action was occurring.[6]

The arrival of the *Graf Spee* required much more than this shoestring set-up, effective though it was within its limitations. Garland recruited his friends and colleagues to help out, Mr Shaw from Montevideo and Messrs Field and Horton from Buenos Aires. Six Marconi radio operators just liberated from the *Graf Spee*, MacDonald from *Streonshalh*, McCorry from *Huntsman*, Guthrie from *Ashlea*, Martinson from *Trevanion*, Comber from *Doric Star* and Prior from *Newton Beech* were also mobilised to provide a comprehensive watch. On 14 December, at the request of Harwood, it was arranged that the regular transmissions from Cerrito should be increased to one every two hours, on the even hours G.M.T. Cerrito cable company operatives had been trained by the British, and money was provided to make sure they gave the British messages due priority – but goodwill was an important factor also. Garland later wrote that he could not speak too highly of the 'co-operation' he had 'received from the Uruguayan telegraphists at Cerrito and the G.P.O. (General Post Office) in Montevideo'.[7] The British merchant ship *Linton Grange* was set up to act as an auxiliary emergency radio station if required (according to neutrality regulations, ships' radios were sealed out of action in port). It was arranged that the signal that *Graf Spee* had sailed would be sent at two frequencies to ensure reception. The system at Montevideo saved a great deal of time. Radio propagation conditions in the South Atlantic were far from optimal and it had taken an hour for Harwood's 'most immediate', calling for *Cumberland*, to be picked up; and another half-hour for it to be made fully clear. Garland estimated that the Montevideo station saved on average five and a half hours in communications time.

At 2200 hrs on the 14th, just as HMS *Cumberland* took up station between *Achilles* and *Ajax*, Langsdorff briefed his officers in *Graf Spee*'s wardroom. He was pessimistic about his chances of being allowed to remain in Montevideo and said he would break the blockade at night to take advantage of poor visibility. He could not allow *Graf Spee* to be interned, as the pro-British Uruguayans would confiscate her and give her to the enemy. The officers seemed unconvinced as to their chances, as they were subject to observation from the British ships in the port and from British intelligence ashore. Langsdorff listened to them and made it clear that at this stage he did not wish to destroy the ship without engaging the enemy first. The idea was also mooted of sailing across the Plate to Buenos Aires to present the friendlier Argentines with a latter-day *Goeben*. This could not however be done directly because of shallows in the estuary and would necessitate action with any Allied units at the mouth of the Plate.

Langsdorff also drafted a terse report for Berlin that he dispatched in the early hours of the following morning. In it, he justified engaging the cruisers, as shaking them off had appeared to be impossible following his attack on the supposed convoy escort. He accounted for the limited success of his own shooting by the problems of ammunition supply to the secondary armament and the need to manœuvre sharply to avoid being hit. Breaking out to the open sea without being shadowed by the cruisers was impossible. He summarised the damage to the galleys, the contaminated flour store and the hit on the forecastle threatening North Atlantic seakeeping.

He mentioned the shell that had pierced the armour belt and tears to the armoured deck, as well as damage to the after part of the ship. As the ship could not be made seaworthy for a breakthrough to Germany with the means on board, he had decided therefore to go into the River Plate, 'at risk of being shut in there'.[8] There was no indication of his intentions at that stage, presumably because the policy of his hosts was still uncertain.

The next day, Friday 15 December, saw feverish work carried out on board *Graf Spee* to repair as much action damage as possible in the expectation of having to give battle to superior forces in the uncomfortably near future. The port number three 5.9-in. gun was fully repaired and the damaged 4.1-in. mount fitted with a British sight captured from the *Newton Beech*. This could now be used against surface targets, if not aircraft. More troublesome were the repairs to the forecastle as steel plates were not available from the shore.

That morning Langsdorff mustered what crew could be spared to bury *Graf Spee*'s dead. The Uruguayan Government allowed the sailors to go ashore. The coffins were lowered over the side at morning divisions to be transferred by tug. The ceremony was attended, contrary to German wishes, by some of the British merchant captains. The inscription on their wreath, 'To the memory of brave men of the sea from their comrades of the British merchant service', was however noted as the act of chivalry it was, and Langsdorff silently saluted his former prisoners. Much was made of Langsdorff's use at this ceremony of the Naval rather than the Nazi salute used by the German civilians present (including the clergy!) but this was quite normal. The Nazi salute was only adopted by the Kriegsmarine later in the war.

That morning too, a slightly embarrassed Millington-Drake informed Guani of the sailing of the *Ashworth* at 1815 hrs that evening and asked, in accordance with the Hague Convention, that *Graf Spee* be prevented from leaving for twenty-four hours afterwards. Guani was genuinely surprised by the change of British tack and commented upon it. He did not let it change his policy towards *Graf Spee*, however, and the Presidential decree calling on *Graf Spee* to depart by 2000 hrs on the 17th was communicated to the German Legation, who received it at about 1200. It is not quite clear when Langsdorff received the depressing news, which must have come as a major blow, particularly in the context of the funeral. He visited Campos with Langmann and other officers during the afternoon, but the subject was formal thanks for the participation of the Uruguayan navy in the morning's events and the offer of hospital facilities. The Minister of Defence said that the rest of *Graf Spee*'s wounded were welcome to be treated ashore and that a German speaking officer would act as liaison. The meeting was held in a correct rather than cordial atmosphere.

The German captain was feeling the pressure. The Germans were imagining all sorts of menaces off Montevideo. On the 15th, the imaginative Ascher thought he spotted the carrier *Ark Royal* and an escort of three destroyers. Like *Renown*, she was nowhere near the Plate at the time but they made a plausible force – and a fatal threat. *Ark Royal* could find and disable *Graf Spee* at long range (especially with the Panzerschiff's reduced A.A. armament) and *Renown* could easily sink her with her 15-in. guns. There were rumours of other ships too, notably *Dunkerque*, whose arrival was mentioned by Uruguayan radio. More correctly, the heavy cruiser *Cumberland* was also reported to the Germans by their friends ashore as being present off the port.

On receipt of the decree, Langsdorff signalled his perceived predicament to Raeder. He stated that *Renown* and *Ark Royal* were indeed off Montevideo, together with cruisers and destroyers. These forces were mounting a 'close blockade at night' and there was 'no prospect of breaking out into the open sea and getting through to Germany'. He intended to try to use the cover of neutral waters to break through to Buenos Aires using his remaining ammunition to fight his way over. However, as: 'a breakthrough might result in the destruction of the *Spee* without the possibility of damage to the enemy', Langsdorff then requested instructions as to whether he should scuttle the ship (in spite of the inadequate depth of water in the Plate estuary) or submit to internment?[9]

The ammunition situation was now a major concern for Langsdorff. It seems probable that initial reports had reassured him that he still had 324 11-in. rounds left after the battle.[10] His final shots against the British cruisers expended some 36 rounds, making a total expenditure in action of 414. His total holdings of 11-in. were however only 600, not the 702 originally thought, and this meant he only had 186 shells left for his main armament, 170 armour-piercing and 16 bottom-fused H.E. (all 200 nose-fused H.E. rounds had been expended).[11] This was only enough for about forty minutes' action, and his experience of 13 January did not give him much confidence in making his shots count. Crucially, although some of its wiring had been repaired, it was impossible to repair the lens of the main rangefinder on the foretop, which was *Graf Spee*'s key instrument. This would make accurate fire even more difficult, especially in any kind of heavy seas. This puts Langsdorff's comment about the possibility of causing damage to the enemy into its proper context.

Langsdorff was also very concerned about the condition of *Graf Spee*'s engines. Indeed, these had become another most critical problem. The diesels had been in action for twice the permissible period without overhaul and, after the stress of the action, there were ominous cracks in the cylinders. The piston rods were out of true and Langsdorff's engineers could not now guarantee speeds of over 17 knots. Combined with his gunnery deficiencies these mechanical difficulties made even a dash to Buenos Aires look problematical in the extreme.

Langmann was more pessimistic even than Langsdorff. In a telegram to Berlin, he argued that an urgent decision was required, reference the pocket battleship. Superior British forces had: 'been quite clearly established from on board *Spee*.' It was clear to Langsdorff, therefore, that it was: 'quite out of the question to shake off shadowers and thus achieve a successful breakthrough to Germany'.[12] The desired stay of fourteen days would only make the situation worse by assisting in enemy concentration of force. The worst possible solution was internment, something with which his

Naval Attaché agreed. 'It would be preferable', he concluded significantly, 'in view of her shortage of ammunition to blow her up in the shallow waters of the Plate and have the crew interned'.[13]

The German Foreign Ministry replied that they found the Uruguayan answer incomprehensible given Spee's reported condition. Langmann and Langsdorff were ordered to try to extend the time limit and to counter the influence of the British as much as they could. That evening they saw Guani, who had just previously received Millington-Drake. The British Minister was ushered out through a side door to avoid the Germans in the ante-room. Despite his recognition that the British, too, wanted the Germans to stay longer, Guani took his stand on neutrality and his Commission's report. The deadline stood.

****

Off the Plate, the three cruisers patrolled their stations, watching for the breakout. Before the arrival of *Cumberland*, the crews of *Ajax* and *Achilles* were very aware of their limited firepower, only one and a half ship's equivalent; and that they too had fired off most of their ammunition. *Achilles* had only some thirty per cent of her complement of shells, *Ajax*, with half her armament knocked out, about fifty per cent. The arrival of the fully stocked and armed heavy cruiser was welcome indeed, although potentially to act only as another *Exeter*. Fuel was also running low on the light cruisers; and on the 15th, Harwood ordered the Royal Fleet Auxiliary *Olynthus* to San Borombon Bay to fuel his ships. He proceeded there with *Ajax* with *Cumberland* covering to the northward in case the pocket battleship appeared. He took 200 tons from the tanker in less than co-operative weather conditions and then went back to join the heavy cruiser. Although kept well-informed by the officers in Montevideo, Harwood could not feel certain that *Graf Spee* would not try a break-out at any moment.

At 1035 hrs on 15 December, Harwood signalled his plans. His object, he tersely stated, was 'destruction'.[14] By this, Harwood meant, of course, of the pocket battleship – but at least one waggish officer who saw the signal said he was not sure to whom the Commodore was referring! This meant his cruisers would have to concentrate, even if that increased the risk of the Germans escaping. *Achilles* was to watch north of English Bank and *Cumberland* to the west, showing herself off Montevideo. If *Graf Spee* left before 2100 (Z plus 2) hrs, the ships in touch were to shadow at maximum range while all units concentrated on the shadower. If the *Graf Spee* had not left by 2100, the ships were to concentrate anyway 15 miles due south of San Antonio, by 0030 hrs. If the German ship left after sunset, *Cumberland* was to launch an aircraft to locate and shadow for as long as possible. If things went wrong, all units were to concentrate at 36° N, 52° W at 0600 hrs. He also reiterated his engagement plan with *Cumberland*'s name substituted for *Exeter*'s.

That evening, McCall went out by boat to try to find out what the Uruguayans had done to detain the Panzerschiff. He was rather disturbed to find that the only thing keeping her in Uruguay was a small tug with a petty officer (armed with a pistol) and four ratings. The attaché thought it necessary to anchor ships around *Graf Spee* to make it essential for her to manœuvre with tugs to leave and tried to contact the Uruguayan Defence Minister, with whom McCall was on good terms, to suggest it to him. Campos, diplomatically, was unavailable for interview. McCall then asked Millington-Drake to request an emergency meeting with Guani at 2330 hrs to ask that a picket be put on board *Graf Spee* to prevent her following a British merchant ship out of harbour. Guani, after some persuasion, telephoned to ask Campos if this could be done but the Defence Minister refused, saying the existing guardship arrangement was adequate. Guani again commented on the interesting change in British approach that now wanted *Graf Spee* to stay. McCall left rather despondently and spent the next few hours with Miller thinking about how they could prevent *Graf Spee* leaving. Sabotage to her screws and rudder was considered but ruled out for diplomatic and political reasons.

Aboard *Graf Spee* repairs went on as best they could under bright lights that lit up the whole harbour. Langsdorff confided to some men that he would attempt a break-out only if it stood some chance of success. He was not going to expend the ship as target practice for the enemy.

Early on the morning of the 16th, Harwood received permission from London that he could engage *Graf Spee* anywhere outside the three-mile limit and thus ignore local claims to the Plate waters. Shortly before, the three cruisers had rendezvoused, as ordered. As they closed the Plate towards dawn, an exhausted Lewin took up *Ajax*'s Seafox to reconnoitre Montevideo from outside the three-mile limit. The tired-out crew reported they had been fired upon in the mist and that they had not been able to confirm *Graf Spee*'s presence in harbour. It was assumed that the ship was making a breakout and the cruisers went to action stations. Then a report arrived confirming *Graf Spee*'s true position, in port. Harwood reported the apparent firing to Montevideo in the hope that an investigation might cause further delay, but the British legation replied that *Graf Spee* had definitely not been the culprit. If there had been firing it was probably from the Argentine guard ship in the area.

Next morning, Harwood welcomed McCall, who had come out in a small tug from a nearby village. The attaché found the Commodore looking: 'tired and haggard', but still 'his usual forceful, charming, imperturbable self'.[15] He learned of *Cumberland*'s arrival, but that *Renown* and *Ark Royal* were still in Brazilian waters a thousand miles away. Given that *Ajax* had only half her 6-in. guns in action, Harwood asked McCall to try to keep *Graf Spee* in harbour for as long as possible. The Commodore also showed his local sensitivity by expressing concern that his orders from London called on him to ignore the territorial sea claims of the locals, claims backed up by all the other American states. Harwood did not want to do anything that would dissipate the most valuable local goodwill that he had helped build up in the preceding years.

These diplomatic concerns, coupled with lack of sea room and the possibility of shells fired over the target landing in Uruguay, decided

Harwood not to engage too close to the coast. At 1515 hrs he signalled this latest appreciation to his units. The object of 'destruction' meant keeping the force together.[16] He would now rely on the shore organisation, whose effectiveness he now fully respected after McCall's visit. *Cumberland*'s Walrus aircraft would be flown off as soon as word of *Graf Spee*'s sailing was received from Montevideo, to acquire the target and make reconnaissance reports. The possible enemy courses were north of English Bank, between the English and Rouen Banks and between the Rouen bank and San Antonio with the extra possibility of doubling back from one to another. Harwood ruled out fighting off Whistle Buoy because of political difficulties. If fighting at dawn, he wanted to keep the advantage of light by moving to the east and engaging the enemy as time and information allowed. The cruisers were not to go too far east as they had to keep within reach of catching the ship on any of the routes, including if the pocket battleship doubled back. *Cumberland* had to be able to use all her armament from the start and the two Divisions were therefore to work eight cables apart with *Achilles* close astern *Ajax.* Once the action began, Divisions were to have complete freedom of action as before. Harwood was not optimistic about being able to catch the German; he put his chances at only thirty per cent.

Morale aboard the British ships was improved early that evening when Harwood received a signal from the First Lord of the Admiralty, Winston Churchill, informing him of his promotion to Rear Admiral, backdated to the day of the battle. He was also informed of the award of a Knight Commander of the Order of the Bath (KCB); his three captains were elevated to Companions of the same order (CB). In communicating this news to his ships, Harwood stressed that all the men had shared in the senior officers' awards.

Ashore, the German mood became still darker and the atmosphere more menacing. On the morning of the 16th, in accordance with his orders from Berlin, Langmann went back to see Campos to try to obtain an extension but received an answer which seemed to the German only to demonstrate the Minister's pro-British sympathies and his primary responsibility for the Presidential decree. In fact, Campos was just sustaining the neutrality of his country from both sides in the war.

At Miller's suggestion, the British also began deception operations to make the Germans think that British heavy units were indeed in the vicinity. Using MI6 channels Miller obtained approval within four hours from London. It was known that the line between Montevideo and Buenos Aires was tapped, so McCall rang Sir Edmond Ovey, the ambassador to Argentina. As McCall later remembered, he told Ovey that:

> I had a message of extreme urgency. He at once cautioned me not to use the telephone, but I replied that the message was so urgent that we would have to risk security, there being no time to encode what I had to say. I thereupon told him that the Admiralty had asked for arrangements to be made for 2,000 tons of fuel oil to be available that evening at Mar del Plata, the Argentine naval base for two of our capital ships. Being exceedingly quick on the uptake, Sir Esmond asked me to repeat the message slowly. He then told my assistant, Commander Lloyd Hirst, to get on with the job . . .[17]

Hirst sought an interview with the pro-German Admiral Scasso in the Ministry of Marine. Coyly, he asked that if *Renown* and *Ark Royal* arrived at Mar del Plata in a day or so, was the entrance deep enough for them to enter, were there tugs big enough to deal with them and could they be berthed and fuelled? As it happened, a senior officer from that very port was in the building and he was called to answer the questions. Sure enough, the Buenos Aires evening press that night contained reports from 'well-informed sources' that the two British ships were due at Mar del Plata within forty-eight hours.

In a formal note on the 15th, Millington-Drake had asked the Uruguayans to prevent the conveyance of 'outside workmen and extraneous material' to *Graf Spee*. On the morning of the following day, he argued that the presence of such workers from ashore was a basis for internment. He followed this up that evening by a rather strongly worded note which drew Guani's attention to the: 'unfortunate situation that would arise if His Majesty's Government were to consider such a conveyance *failing subsequent internment of the ship by the Uruguayan authorities* (my italics) constituted a breach of Uruguayan neutrality.'[18] *Graf Spee* should, Millington-Drake requested, be detained pending an investigation. Understandably, given the different pressures he had been under, Guani became annoyed but said there would be a thorough investigation, handing the note to a Secretary for attention. He also put in a telephone call to the Inspector General of Marine to stop movements of workmen to the ship. Somewhat bitterly, he took refuge in Pan-American unity; complaining that all of America resented being drawn into European quarrels, and that joint action was being considered to avoid a repeat battle in South American waters.

Millington-Drake defended himself by claiming that *Graf Spee* had fired first in every encounter close to shore – a fact hotly disputed by the observing Uruguayan warship – and that the cruisers were only defending the French liner *Formose*, an even broader version of the truth. Millington-Drake then tried Guani's patience beyond endurance by handing over a note reporting the sailing of the *Dunster Grange* and again asking that *Graf Spee* be detained another twenty-four hours for safety after the British ship had left harbour. 'After a short laugh, Dr Guani became quite angry and spoke to me as if to a naughty schoolboy, saying that on no account was I to repeat this manœuvre as it would give the *Graf Spee* an excuse to prolong her stay. She was: "a most unwelcome guest" and was to be got rid of as soon as possible'.[19] All merchant ship sailings from the port were being suspended from 2000 hrs that night. At a stroke, this ruling deflated the British 'twenty-four hour rule' strategy. *Graf Spee* had to sail the following evening, but in a narrow window between the time twenty-four hours after the *Dunster Grange* actually cleared the harbour and the expiry of the Uruguayan ultimatum. This would help the British prevent an escape.

Down at the harbour another little drama was being played out that had a considerable impact on Langsdorff. The workmen and steel plate required to repair the hole in *Graf Spee*'s bows had arrived, but the Uruguayans would not let them on board. This was not the high-level response to Millington-Drake's protests and Guani's phone call that he imagined, but the result of the chartering by *Graf Spee*'s contractor, Ribereña, of a Port Authority launch to take the men and their materials to *Graf Spee*. The harbour authorities felt this compromised Uruguayan neutrality too much and insisted the government launch had to be replaced by a private vessel. Langsdorff was infuriated by the delay to the work required to repair the most significant damage to his ship and suspected the Montevideo government of deliberate obstruction. A diplomat was sent to the Foreign Ministry to sort out the situation, but after about an hour the new launch took the repair party aboard. This little affair was of no real significance in itself but in the highly charged atmosphere in *Graf Spee* it added considerably to Langsdorff's gloom; the authorities in Montevideo seemed to be making vital repairs impossible. In reality, the President had overruled Guani and allowed *Graf Spee* to continue to make repairs.

Just as the workmen were being barred from *Graf Spee*, Langmann met Guani. In an extended and heated interview lasting over an hour the German minister demanded enough time for negotiations over the *Graf Spee* issue. If such time was not granted, the ship would be blown up spectacularly just off his capital. Langmann made it clear that he held Guani responsible for the situation and requested an audience with President Baldomir. Guani countered by saying the matter could not be referred to higher authority unless the Germans promised to abide without question by its decision, whatever it was. In the absence of such an undertaking *Graf Spee* had to leave Montevideo by 2000 hrs the following evening or she would be interned.

Millington-Drake had asked for another interview later in the evening and it was a tribute to his relationship with Guani that this was granted, at 2100 hrs. The British minister found Guani in a calmer and more friendly mood. Obviously, standing up to Langmann had sublimated the Uruguayan's aggression. Guani repeated what Langmann had said. He had been worried by Langmann's threatening attitude and the possibility of German action against the 'almost unarmed' Uruguay. He had therefore appealed to other American countries and had received statements of sympathy and support. The American ambassador had been in to see him twice and he was in constant touch with Buenos Aires. Guani asked Millington-Drake therefore not to press him too hard, as he 'was on the point of aligning all the nations of the American continent against Germany.'[20]

Guani had clearly been very upset by the Germans and was now willing to go further than at any time previously to help the British. When Millington-Drake asked for internment or a small delay, Guani (as Millington-Drake reported to London): 'at once said that if that was so and there were mutual confidence between us, it would be helpful that he should after all give a small extension which might just be sufficient for the British purpose. He asked me to consult you and reply informally if possible tomorrow, Sunday at about 11.00 a.m. (1630 hrs British time). Further, whereas the Minister had told me at 5.30 that he was preventing any merchant ship from sailing after 8.00 p.m., he now said that it might after all be convenient if we sent out a merchant vessel daily.'[21] The Houlder meat ship *Duquesa* bound for Buenos Aires had been held up by the port closure and was next in line to be sent out to delay *Graf Spee*, under the twenty-four hour rule

This was vitally important news. When he returned to the legation, Millington-Drake heard from McCall that the big British ships were not due until the 19th at the earliest. He then composed a cable, No. 165, from which the above excerpts are quoted, but this was not sent until 0502 hrs the following morning, being logged in the Foreign Office at 1020 on the 17th. This seems very odd, considering the urgency of the situation. It was a Saturday night/Sunday morning which might have imposed, even in wartime, limitations on either the cyphering or sending or even perhaps the potential receiving and deciphering of a particularly sensitive telegram. In these circumstances, Millington-Drake may have been waiting to see if *Graf Spee* sailed early on the 17th. He had received, as he told London, from a 'good source', information that *Graf Spee* would sail between 0300 and 0500 hrs to take advantage of the morning mist.[22] The telegram did go out, very shortly after it was clear *Graf Spee* was not going to sail.

It took some hours for the reply to be processed and it therefore missed the Uruguayans' deadline. Not till 1630 hrs on the 17th, the time Millington-Drake should have been referring back to Guani, could the Foreign Office telegraph back to Montevideo the news that: 'Admiralty would prefer *Graf Spee* should not sail before Wednesday morning December 20th. Up till then any delay is to our advantage.'[23] It is not known if Millington-Drake tried to have an audience with Guani before or after receiving this telegram on the morning of the 17th. He may have made the attempt, as he admits to having had foreknowledge of the meeting Guani had that afternoon with the Pan-American ambassadors. It would seem strangely out of character for the energetic British minister not to have taken taken some pains to exploit Guani's remarkable offer of the previous evening, even without a reply from London. A request for the opening of the port for the the departure of the *Duquesa* would have been appropriate.

Perhaps Millington-Drake was impressed by Guani's transmission of Langmann's threat that the *Graf Spee* would be blown up rather than make a run for it? In these circumstances it was less vital to hold the ship in Montevideo. Perhaps he did make some representations, only to receive a rebuff as Guani had changed his mind in the cold light of dawn and had reverted to taking refuge in Pan-American solidarity that demanded strict neutrality? We do not know, as Millington-Drake was very reticent indeed about this incident. The part of telegram 165 of 16/17 January quoted above, together with its reply, is notably absent from his book (other parts of 165 are quoted). In a letter to the Foreign Office Librarian in 1962, he admitted having: 'deliberately left out a paragraph in which there is a hint of collusion between Dr Guani and myself on that Saturday evening, especially as nothing came of it.'[24]

But why did nothing come of it? Millington-Drake no doubt wished to protect Guani from accusations of un-neutral conduct, as he was always anxious to praise the Foreign Minister's role. It is all a little mysterious; but, in fact, the die had already been cast. As Millington-Drake and Guani had conferred on the Saturday evening, in terms that might have eased a little of the pressure on Langsdorff – but in effect would have truly sealed his fate – a crucial decision had just been taken at the German legation. This would lead to the spectacular denouement of the crisis the following evening.

CHAPTER EIGHT

Scuttled

The morning of Saturday 16 December saw a crisis meeting of Grossadmiral Raeder and his most trusted staff officers. The subject was the *Graf Spee*. Raeder, who must have been frustrated at Langsdorff having landed himself in a very predictable mess, reported the situation as signalled to him from the Panzerschiff. The supposed stationing of *Renown* and *Ark Royal* off the Plate seemed to make a break-out to Germany hopeless. Fregattenkapitän Wagner of the Operations Branch disagreed with Langsdorff's pessimistic appreciation. Based on intelligence sources, he argued (correctly, as it happened) that it was impossible for the heavy units to be off the Plate. Admiral Schniewind, the Chief of Staff, overruled him. Langsdorff as the man on the spot knew better than Berlin did: if he had seen the battlecruiser and the carrier, then they were there. Raeder, who was scheduled to see Hitler at 1300 hrs, then decided, in accordance with his general policy of leaving the final decisions to the man on the spot, to recommend not setting specific instructions on *Graf Spee*'s fate, other than ruling out internment at Montevideo.[1]

Raeder duly reported the situation to the Führer, telling him that two weeks were needed to make *Graf Spee* seaworthy but the Uruguayans would only grant seventy-two hours. The Foreign Ministry was being requested to continue its efforts to obtain an extension, but this seemed hopeless as a result of Allied pressure. Uruguay, he said, was 'unreliable as a neutral' and unable to defend her neutrality. *Graf Spee*'s internment there was therefore 'out of the question'. A breakout to 'stronger' Argentina was therefore worthy of consideration as this would permit greater freedom of action. Langsdorff had proposed such a breakout but had requested a decision as to whether, if the prospect was hopeless, he should accept internment or scuttle the ship in the fairly shallow waters of the La Plata river. He then quoted Langsdorff's signal, before concluding that he could not recommend internment in Uruguay. The 'right course' would be 'an attempt to break through, or, if necessary, to scuttle the ship in the La Plata river.' Hitler agreed. He too opposed internment in Uruguay: 'especially since there is a possibility that the *Graf Spee* might score a success against the British ships in the break-out.' He 'entirely approved' of Raeder's instructions to Langsdorff. These left open the scuttling option, but it is clear the Führer was far from reconciling himself as yet to the destruction of his Panzerschiff.[2]

A signal along these lines was composed after the meeting and sent at 1707 hrs. It ordered Langsdorff to attempt by all means to extend his ship's time in neutral waters, 'in order to guarantee freedom of action for as long as possible'. It approved his signalled intention to attempt a possible breakout to Buenos Aires using a combination of neutral waters and available ammunition. As for the request for instructions regarding the options of scuttling or internment, Raeder, with some emphasis, ruled out the latter option. Scuttling was not ordered; but if it was resorted to, 'effective destruction' was to be attempted.[3] Hitler and Raeder had narrowed Langsdorff's realistic options to two; breakout to Argentina, or the effective self-immolation of his ship.

In a supplementary reply to Langsdorff's signal, the German Foreign Ministry had demurred at believing in *Ark Royal*'s presence off the Plate as it was convinced she had already been sunk. 'By order of the Führer', it commanded that an attempt be made to photograph the ship and the pictures sent to Berlin.[4] This caused some frustration in Montevideo as the ship had only been 'sighted' on the horizon. Nevertheless, the attempt was made. Wattenberg hired a small sports plane; however, the pilot insisted that the Plate was out of bounds to all flights. He took up the German officer, but flew instead over land at some distance from the coast. Wattenberg 'could not observe the waters of the estuary, let alone any ship on them.'[5] To add to his frustrations, Wattenberg had to wait some time for a launch back to the ship, where he found that all secret documents had now been destroyed. Various important items such as the ensign flown in the battle and the damaged picture of Admiral Spee had been sent ashore. It was not an encouraging sign, although work went on to repair damage and provisioning from the *Tacoma* also continued.

The signal from Berlin arrived in Montevideo shortly after midday. Langsdorff agonised over the alternatives. He thought that the time allowed by the Uruguayans was insufficient to patch *Graf Spee*'s hull sufficiently to make her capable of an ocean voyage. The ammunition remaining was also insufficient for a long voyage home, even if *Graf Spee* broke out successfully – an action that might exhaust available shells anyway. Coming out of the Plate at slow speed, *Graf Spee* would be at a severe gunnery disadvantage with her foretop rangefinder out of action and only her three unreliable forward guns bearing. She might well be hit, perhaps by a torpedo, a threat of which Langsdorff was acutely conscious, especially in the restricted waters of the Plate where manœuvring was difficult. If she took water, and her draught was increased, *Graf Spee* would go aground and be smashed to a hulk by a heavy British bombardment. The abandoned wreck could then be captured and *Graf Spee*'s secret equipment would fall into enemy hands. If *Graf Spee* tried to prolong her stay against Uruguay's will, the Germans considered that it was not impossible that the British might be allowed into Montevideo harbour to deal with the pocket battleship, with, again, the possible capture of the ship and disastrous results for German–Uruguayan relations as the inevitable outcome.

He conferred with his officers. Nerves were on edge and discussions were sometimes heated. The breakout to Buenos Aires was dismissed after consultations with Wattenberg, Hopfner, the ship's navigation officer, and Klepp, the Engineering officer. Hopfner and Klepp were particularly anxious about the navigational and engineering threats.

The cooling water intakes on *Graf Spee*'s bottom might be clogged by the muddy waters, the engines might run hot and the ship, helpless, be reduced to a wreck, with the same associated dangers of capture as before. It was also by no means certain that Buenos Aires would offer a more welcoming approach than Montevideo. Moreover, once there, the long and winding channel to the Argentine capital would make a surprise breakout impossible.[6]

Langsdorff later conferred with Ascher, Diggins his flag lieutenant and Niebuhr. The depressing logic pointed in one direction, to scuttling in such a way that the destruction of the ship's secret equipment would be ensured. Preparations to scuttle were to be made at once; but the decision was as yet only tentative. Grasping at straws, Langsdorff delayed a final decision until after the German Minister had made one last attempt to extend the ship's stay. Langsdorff communicated the news to the ship's company mustered on the quarterdeck. Then, at 1930 hrs, Langsdorff went ashore to the German legation. Here he met Langmann, fresh from his difficult interview with Guani. There would be no time extension. Quickly, according to Niebuhr, Langsdorff made up his mind that scuttling *Graf Spee* was his only option. Berlin had been informed of Langmann's failure and, in a signal that was decoded by about 2040 hrs, Raeder's approval of the options of breakout or thorough self-destruction were confirmed. This effectively authorised Langsdorff to proceed.

Together with Niebuhr, Langmann, the Legation Secretary Dr F. Rademacher and a shipping company friend of Langmann's, Sanstede (perhaps an intelligence officer working under cover), the Germans planned the actions consequent on Langsdorff's fatal decision.[7] First, the Naval Attaché telegraphed Buenos Aires for tugs to take the *Graf Spee*'s ship's company to Argentina. Discussions were also held on how many of *Graf Spee*'s officers might remain in Montevideo to be appointed to German embassies in South America. Next, an open letter was composed, to be transmitted to the Uruguayan authorities and to be published in the press over Langsdorff's signature. It began by thanking the people of Uruguay for their 'innumerable demonstrations of sympathy', and for their 'chivalrous sentiments' towards the German dead and wounded. Diplomatically, it also thanked the Uruguayan authorities for their 'prompt measures of help taken from the moment of the unexpected arrival of the *Graf Spee* and for the very effective assistance given to my wounded and the honours rendered to my dead.'

However, the tone soon changed, as the letter went on to protest that: 'amidst these demonstrations of true human sentiments a jarring note was struck.' This referred to the Uruguayans' 'final and binding' decision, communicated to Langmann that evening, to insist on *Graf Spee* sailing by 2000 hrs on 17 December, even if necessary repairs had not been completed. Under the Hague convention, ships were allowed to remain in neutral harbours to complete repairs essential to safe navigation, and Langsdorff/Langmann pointed to the extended period of several weeks for such repairs granted to HMS *Glasgow* at Rio in 1914. After an 'expert survey' of the ship, Langsdorff said, he had asked the Uruguayans for fifteen days to repair the damage that had 'compromised the seaworthiness' of *Graf Spee*. The Uruguayan commission of experts had appreciated that the time was not needed to repair the ship's fighting capacity, as the armament and engines had 'suffered to such a little extent' (something of an untruth). However, they had seen the damage to the hull, repair of which was 'essential to the seaworthiness of the vessel.' It had also been 'patently obvious' to the commission that the cooking installations on board had been damaged, and that it was 'essential (considering the large crew borne) that these installations be in good order before a long period on the high seas could be contemplated'. The Uruguayan commission had only allowed seventy-two hours to complete the work. 'In spite of strenuous efforts', the letter went on, it had not been possible to complete the work in such a short time. This could have been ascertained 'beyond all doubt at any time, if a further investigation had been carried out on board.' The letter then complained formally about the workmen not being allowed aboard that afternoon 'for a space of some hours' – but made no mention of the problems of protocol which the Uruguayan authorities had had in allowing the men to be transferred in a neutral ship.

The decision of the Uruguayans was compelling Langsdorff, he complained, 'to leave the harbour of Montevideo with a ship which could not be sufficiently repaired to ensure the maximum safety of navigation. To put to sea in such a vessel would be to bring danger upon my crew (over 1,000 men) by negligence. When I say "danger", I do not mean such danger as would be involved in an action with the enemy. I am referring exclusively to the danger that would inevitably menace a ship at sea in such a condition.' The decision was 'a flagrant violation of the efforts to humanise warfare.' It was hard to account for the difference between the attitude of the Uruguayan people and their government, said Langsdorff, but it was almost certainly down to 'external pressure'. *Graf Spee*'s captain then mentioned darkly that he had 'abstained carefully' from applying such pressure himself, 'although it would have been within my technical possibilities'.

'Langsdorff's' letter then briefly described the action on the 13th, emphasising the Captain's respect for the waters claimed by the littoral states. This had caused him to 'abstain from further part in the action, despite favourable tactical circumstances'. It was also claimed that Langsdorff had deliberately abstained from engaging 'the British cruiser standing off the Isla de Lobos until the enemy had fired on my ship and shot had fallen close'. He concluded:

> I do not recognise the grounds for the decision of the Government of Uruguay – nevertheless I shall respect the time limit imposed. Inasmuch as the government of Uruguay refused to grant me time to make my ship seaworthy as laid down in the Hague convention, I am not minded to place my ship (which has suffered no diminution of its fighting power during the action) under the control of that Government. Under these circumstances I have no alternative but to sink my ship. I shall blow her up close inshore and disembark my crew if this may be possible.[8]

It is hard to accept this statement completely at face value. It was intended as a political document and one can detect in it the hand of Langmann, Rademacher and Stanstede. It contained a number of inaccuracies and overstatements. The emphasis on his forbearance and respect for Uruguayan waters would have been hotly contested by Harwood and his captains. The situation was not as favourable to *Graf Spee* as Langsdorff claimed. HMS *Glasgow* had spent only a week in dry dock at Rio between Coronel and the Falklands and the workmen had been delayed perhaps for an hour or so. They had immediately set to work, and the vital hole in the bows was soon covered. The equally vital auxiliary boiler was also repaired by Saturday evening; so, although the galleys seem still to have been inoperative, it was hardly true that the *Graf Spee* was as unfit for sea as Langsdorff was claiming. The major holes had all been patched in the time available. Heavy weather might have re-opened some of them, but it is hard to see how more time would have helped. The decision to scuttle, as explained above, had a broader rationale and had much more to do with *Graf Spee*'s reduced fighting power – which Langsdorff understated – and the threat supposedly at the mouth of the Plate. There was no mention of ammunition shortages or an inoperative main rangefinder. The emphasis on a split between Uruguayan government and people was also more propaganda than anything else. Although the citizens of Montevideo had shown respect at the funeral of the German sailors, police had had to hold back hostile crowds whenever launches from *Graf Spee* arrived at the quayside. Langsdorff knew about German unpopularity in Uruguay. His letter, with its veiled remark about the possible application of 'pressure' on Uruguay, presumably to be taken as a threat to bombard the capital with his 11-in. guns, only increased that unpopularity when it was published after the scuttling.

Niebuhr called the German embassy in Buenos Aires to obtain the services of the Hamburg South America Line's tugs to pick up *Graf Spee*'s crew. Between 0300 and 0400 hrs Langsdorff returned to his Panzerschiff bearing the bad news. Ascher, Wattenberg, Klepp and perhaps one or two others were waiting for him in the wardroom.

Langsdorff dropped his bombshell: *'Das Schiff wird gesprengt'* ('The ship will be blown up').[9] All repair work was to cease forthwith. Instead, as dawn broke, demolition of vital equipment began. At 0450 hrs, Rasenack was awakened and ordered to destroy the fire control system. The thunderstruck officer went to Langsdorff for personal confirmation of this extraordinary instruction, which was duly given.

So he set about his task. 'With hand grenades we blew up the automatic installations of fire control; with hammers we broke the dials of the delicate controls with their electronics... And so on, gadget after gadget. The removable pieces and the gun breeches we take to the big turrets. There we will blow them up together. Towards midday we had concluded our sad duty. What we see around us is terrible... this is the hardest day of my life.'[10]

At 1300 hrs another kind of bombshell hit the German embassy in Montevideo, the news that *Ark Royal* and *Renown* had arrived at Rio. They were not outside Montevideo after all. It was now too late to put the scuttling decision into reverse. In any case, Langsdorff had convinced himself that he had taken the right decision, whatever enemy warships he was facing outside. The sailing of the *Dunster Grange*, late, at 1815 hrs on the 16th, had decisively narrowed his options. He explained his final reasoning two days later to an Argentinean officer in one of the last conversations of his life. *Graf Spee*, he said, was still in a 'precarious condition' and her engines could not withstand navigation in the muddy River Plate waters. As to considering battle with whatever lay outside, he had been obliged to abandon it for the simple reason that the precise limitation of time for going out, between 1815–2000 hrs, made it certain he would have to accept combat in a part of the River Plate where it was so shallow that if, having exhausted his remaining ammunition (only 186 shells for his six big guns, that fired two salvos a minute), he had to scuttle his ship, there was no certainty that it would even sink below the surface of the water. In such conditions, there was always the possibility that the enemy would capture her, refloat her and conduct her in triumph to England.

He was concerned, Langsdorff told the Argentinean, to prevent the British navy from gaining a victory which could afterwards be exploited for political ends. Scuttling with proper preparation, resulting in more complete destruction, was therefore the lesser of the two evils.[11]

The materials and supplies transferred from the *Tacoma* were returned to the German merchantman, which also received some of *Graf Spee*'s remaining provisions. During the afternoon, personnel transfers to the Tacoma began; and, by 1800 hrs, some 900 of *Graf Spee*'s officers and men had been taken off. The Germans tried to keep their activities as covert as possible. Canvas awnings were used to shield what was going on aboard ship from sight and the men were ordered to hide in the hold, away from the public gaze, it being intended to smuggle them out on board the ship to Argentina. It was far from clear what was going on until quite late in the day. The Uruguayans were prepared for every contingency. If the ship did sail, *Uruguay* and *Huracan* would follow at a distance observing *Graf Spee*'s movements in territorial waters and taking note of any action. They were to help with rescue operations if required. If *Graf Spee* was to be interned, she would be placed in Montevideo's Dock B and immobilised. Forty men, as laid down in the Hague Convention, would stay on board to maintain the ship in good condition. The rest of the crew would be interned on Flores island, with the senior officers on parole, as provided for in the Convention. There would, however, have been a serious problem if Langsdorff remained in harbour and refused to give up his ship. Uruguay could not reinforce the order and her navy simply did not have the capability to take on *Graf Spee*. Langsdorff was to be requested to comply with the internment order, and: 'due note would be taken if it were not complied with.'[12] Uruguay's weapons were primarily diplomatic. Guani held a meeting on Sunday afternoon of all the representatives of the American states, to explain his country's position and pave the way for joint hemispheric action should *Graf Spee* prove troublesome. The Brazilians moved their air force to the Uruguayan border in support should the Germans resist internment by force.

At sea, meanwhile, Harwood ordered *Achilles* to fuel from the R.F.A. *Olynthus* with the other two cruisers acting as lookout. The ships then cruised together to the south-east of English Bank, remaining concentrated. Intelligence from Montevideo reported the landing of the borrowed welding equipment, which seemed to presage a breakout attempt. Morale in Harwood's ships remained high as they prepared to renew the battle. Then at 1440 hrs the first news of the personnel transfers was signalled to Harwood.[13] The cruisers also had another source of information in the broadcast voice of an American radio reporter, Mike Fowler, who had set himself up overlooking Montevideo harbour. He had arrived in Montevideo to make programmes about the local bird life but found himself in this very different situation. His broadcasts were listened to with interest aboard the British ships and apparently by President Roosevelt in the U.S.A.

It should be remembered from this distance in time that this was one of the first great 'media events' of the war, with frequent reports on radio and summaries in the daily press. It seemed the eyes of the whole world were on Montevideo that sunny afternoon of December 17, 1940. The waterfront was thronged with spectators from both sides of the Plate, anxious to see the developing situation. The crowds were estimated at three quarters of a million. On board *Graf Spee*, the officers were persuading Langsdorff not to blow himself up with the ship. Ascher ordered Rasenack to arrange the scuttling charges so the process could be started at one point in the ship. Langsdorff wanted to be the last man aboard and immolate himself in one final, defiant gesture. He had argued that captains should never abandon their ship. Ascher disagreed with this view, and used the difficulty of running cables through the ship and the possibility that some charges would not go off to dissuade Langsdorff from his chosen course of action. He persuaded his commanding officer that he had a duty to get the ship's company to Buenos Aires as the enemy, frustrated in their inability to get the *Graf Spee*, might try to capture her crew. Langsdorff thereupon accepted that the ship would be destroyed by separate firing circuits.

Rasenack, Ascher and the Chief Engineer met to plan the destruction of the ship. Six torpedo heads were used to provide the basic scuttling charges. Two seem to have been placed in the loading stations of the 11-in. turrets, suspended with ropes over the ammunition hatches, and the rest in the machinery spaces. Ammunition was piled to add to the effect. The six separate explosions were to be set off by demolition charges carried to destroy captured merchant ships, detonated by a hand grenade cap connected to a battery of accumulators. The detonation of each charge was controlled by a modified chronometer, with all the devices timed to go off simultaneously. To convert each turret into what Rasenack called 'one big explosive charge', the turrets and barbettes were filled with shells and bags of propellant. This, it was hoped, would be enough to initiate major magazine explosions.[14]

One British harbour watcher at least could see through a chink in the German awnings, thus Harwood was informed mid-afternoon that 300–400 men had left *Graf Spee*. Millington-Drake, anxious that Pan-American sensibilities should not be upset, cabled the Foreign Office at 1605 hrs, emphasising the importance of Harwood's ships not opening fire first in waters in the Plate estuary claimed by Uruguay and Argentina. These claims, he had reason to believe, had the support of the governments of all countries of the American continent. This signal went *en clair*, such was its perceived urgency. Secrecy was soon abandoned on the German side also, and at 1720 hrs Harwood learned that over 700 men had been transferred to the *Tacoma* and that it was possible that *Graf Spee* might scuttle herself. Millington-Drake also telegraphed London with the news and the indication it implied that the ship was either going to scuttle herself or attempt with a reduced crew to escape to Buenos Aires for a less hostile internment. He reiterated that in these circumstances it was even more important that Harwood did not fire first in the estuary. He also reported that he had asked the Uruguayans to detain *Tacoma* as she had been effectively converted into a naval auxiliary.

Langsdorff had told the harbour authorities that he intended to leave at or shortly after 1815 hrs. By that time only he and a 'Kommando' of officers and N.C.O.s remained on board, forty-two in all. Shortly after 1800 hrs, a large ensign was broken out on the foremast, together with another on the mainmast. The two anchors were raised in turn and *Graf Spee* began to move, followed by her boats and the Tacoma. Above flew aircraft filming the public spectacle for American newsreels. Strong summer evening sunlight illuminated the dramatic scene. Not many words were spoken on this last voyage of the Panzerschiff as she sailed westwards into the setting sun, out of what her captain called the 'tremendous rat trap' of Montevideo.[15]

Millington-Drake had taken up his position in the flat of Clarence Horton of the Central Uruguayan Railway, in the Palacio Salvo, the tallest building in Montevideo. As he remembered just over ten years later, 'the air was full of the distant noise of crowds, motor car sirens and loudspeakers blaring forth to report what was happening to those who were not situated to view the scene'.[16] In another memoir, he added: 'Countless crowds were watching from every conceivable vantage point, down by the many wharves of the port, on the top of every building and beyond the port on the slopes of the hill, right up to the lighthouse, where actually the President of the Republic, General Baldomir, had gone with Dr Guani to observe what would happen.'[17]

The crowds seemed disappointed when *Graf Spee* turned away from her hunters, clearly seen as smoking objects on the horizon, and turned to starboard as if making for Buenos Aires. About an hour after sailing, she stopped for the last time in position 34°58' S, 56°18' W, just over four miles from the coast. The engine room crew was taken off by one of the ship's launches. One member of *Graf Spee*'s last crew, Chief Engine Room Artificer Hans Gotz, remembered the next dramatic minutes thus:

> Once more and for the last time the alarm bells rang on board. Six torpedo heads had been placed in different parts of the ship and six

> men with iron nerves connected the accumulators to the clock, of which the alarm had been set at twenty minutes to eight (*Graf Spee seems actually to have exploded at 1954 hrs*). Each man with his bag of provisions, his lifebelt and his pistol in his pocket came away with a determined face from the engine room and also from the fore and stern 11-in. turrets, to the upper deck. At the stern there lay the motor boat as planned.[18]

Wattenberg had been tasked by Kay, the executive officer, to look after the captain and prevent him going down with the ship:

> After we had dropped anchor, the alarm clock was set to explode the charges in twenty minutes time . . . So there remained ample time for the various seamen and technical members of the Kommando to get into a launch and make their way to the *Tacoma*. At the very last, we five officers gathered with our Captain on the quarterdeck . . . and then we got into the Captain's launch which had also come alongside. We went about one mile away and then awaited the moment until the fuse should do its work.[19]

Already, the tugs from Buenos Aires, operated under the Argentine flag by the German owned La Porteña company, had appeared, having sailed that morning. They arrived at 1930 hrs to find *Graf Spee* stopped, 'the last rays of the evening sun shining sadly on the beautiful ship', as Captain Hebe, marine superintendent of Hamburg South America and the man in charge of the operation, remembered. There were two tugs, *Coloso* and *Gigante*, the latter towing a barge called *Chiriguеña*. As the tugs closed *Graf Spee*, a launch redirected them to the *Tacoma* with the news that *Graf Spee* would shortly be blown up. This seems to have been the Captain's barge that evacuated the final personnel. Hebe remembered *Graf Spee*'s two flags being hauled down, 'and the launches full of men come away from her quickly as she lay quietly and majestically on the still waters.'

Also observing events closely were the three British cruisers. As *Graf Spee* was about to weigh anchor, Harwood completed what he later called a 'pessimistic and sentimental' letter to his wife which gives a good idea as to his state of mind at this crucial moment:

> Well – Well – Well – what a life – How much I could tell you if allowed and with you – I am very well indeed – I was not touched or nearly so and nobody near me got hit – parts were nasty, damned nasty but on the whole we were never very badly off in Ajax, poor Exeter bought most of the troubles... Things are tricky at the moment as we don't know if he is coming out again – I have a most difficult problem to catch him again and if he escapes then all the good we have done will be upset – not all but a lot of it – The mouth of the Plate is so wide and there are so many ways out that it is very difficult – Probably another battle and who knows – I hope for the best – If yes or no you will know long before you get this. – If the worst happens... – I will write much more later but this is a hurried line in case the worst happens.[20]

A few days later, the newly knighted Sir Henry Harwood wrote a second letter to Lady Harwood, as she now was, with a fuller description of 'that most trying time':

> I hope I shall never be in such a position again – Showered with honours before the job was done, faced with a most difficult problem to intercept her if she broke out, there are so many ways out to a wide mouthed river – Then on intercepting a point blank range battle – Oh Joan – No wonder I was worried – As sunset came on we went to action stations and got ready – I had in my optimistic way always thought she would intern herself, but really could not believe my own luck – Suddenly out of the blue came a signal – *Graf Spee* is transferring men to *Tacoma* – Strange, my optimism returned but caution prevailed – next 3 to 400 men being transferred. Next 700 men – What was up – It must be true – A

> long pause – from the BBC, She has sailed – new anxiety – where gone – BBC, gone up river towards BA – a trap I thought – Long pause going back again – *Tacoma* sailed – Then a report of smoke – vertical smoke, looked like her fore structure – Increase speed, back to action stations – smoke got no nearer. I sent the aircraft up. No report for an interminable time. . . .[21]

At 1954 hrs local time, *Graf Spee* blew up.

There was first a relatively small explosion in the engine room and then a much larger one in the after turret and magazine. A huge column of flame rose from the ship, followed by a mushroom cloud of smoke. The first explosion caused a misfire in the charges in the fore turret. The torpedo head was later found still suspended inside the turret and the forward part of the ship was comparatively undamaged structurally. The after turret was, however, destroyed, its guns being tossed into the air 'like toothpicks', as Rasenack later put it.[22] The charges in the engine room also demolished the central portion of the *Graf Spee*, her funnel being blown over to settle leaning heavily to starboard. Fires, fed by petrol which had been poured over the decks, broke out throughout the wreck and it began to settle in the shallow water with a slight list to starboard. *Graf Spee*'s sea cocks had been opened to speed the sinking The German observers obtained grim satisfaction from the apparent destruction of most, if not all, that was valuable on the ship. The observers ashore were shocked temporarily into silence. In the room high above Montevideo where he was watching with his father, eleven year-old Jim Millington-Drake (who later joined the Royal Navy) piped up, 'Well, that's the end of her.'[23] Harwood's account to his wife continued:

> Suddenly from the aircraft – She has blown herself up. What a relief, cheers from all the quarters – the men poured up on deck. I looked at *Achilles* – her upper deck and turrets were black with men – I told her to take station ahead as we passed – Her N. Zealanders and ours cheered and cheered – I stood on the bridge and wore my

> Admiral's uniform for the 1st time – We all cheered – Like armistice night. . .[24]

Lewin, the Seafox pilot, later remembered:

> Of the actual scuttling, I do not know if the grandstand view which we had from the air was more impressive than it was from the ground, but it was quite Wagnerian. *Graf Spee* was silhouetted against the sun, which to us had not set yet, and the fantastic series of explosions with which she destroyed herself still stick in my mind. On return to the Cruiser quadron, Kearney (the observer) and I were much incensed by being kept waiting until it got darker and darker, and it was not until after we had landed and *Achilles* steamed past in the midst of a mass Maori war dance that we appreciated the very high spirits that our squadron mates were in.[25]

In *Achilles*, as Washbourne remembered shortly afterwards, 'We ordered all hands on deck: and with guns still loaded and tubes inserted, everyone left their quarters and crowded on all the vantage points of the ship to see the last of the old enemy. *Ajax*, leading us, either forgot to make a signal to tell us she had reduced, or we weren't troubling about signals at that time. We shot up on her, sheered out, and, as the two ships passed close to in the gathering there was the most magnificent spontaneous expression of feeling, and each ship cheered until no one had any voice left, and when we stopped through exhaustion someone in *Ajax* shouted , "Well done the Diggers", and it started all over again. I don't expect ever to feel or witness anything like that again.'[26]

As *Graf Spee* blew up, the Argentine vessels closed the *Tacoma*, stopped at the edge of the three-mile limit. They came alongside and the German sailors descended into them by rope ladder. While this transfer was in progress tugs from Montevideo appeared. One was the British owned and commanded *Enriqueta* that had been kept standing by all day at the disposal of the British legation. As the *Graf Spee* exploded, she cast off with Lt A.E. Cassells RN, on the staff of the Marine Department of the Consulate, aboard. She was then hailed by a port official to take him out to witness the sensational events taking place at sea. By the time the tug had closed the *Tacoma*, much of the transfer had taken place. The official on board hailed the tugs and asked under whose instructions they were acting. He was told the vessels were bound for Argentina as instructed by their company. More tugs then appeared from Montevideo, one carrying the senior port official, Señor Riquero, who ordered the tugs not to move away. *Gigante*, barge in tow, made a run for it under the command of Korvettenkapitän Hopfner, *Graf Spee*'s Second Navigating Officer, who used his knowledge of these waters to take a route through shallows close to the Uruguayan coast, before crossing to the Ortiz bank and the normal route to Buenos Aires. *Enriqueta* sailed across the bows of the *Coloso*, which was forced to heave-to. Langsdorff now appeared in his launch and came on board Enriqueta. The tug's skipper, Albert Jack, spoke Spanish; and, after acting the part by speaking poor English with a heavy accent, was taken by Langsdorff to be a Uruguayan. Cassells hid below. Jack poured a 'very tired and nervy' Langsdorff a much-needed whisky.[27] The German insisted that he was outside the Uruguayans' waters and that they had no right to interfere. Argentina had a larger German colony and was better able to look after the interned crews. Uruguay was a small country that would find it harder to support the Germans. A drink was passed to the port official to facilitate negotiations. The Uruguayan insisted that he was not concerned with the sinking of the *Graf Spee* but with the transfer to the tugs and barge.

The Uruguayan gunboat *Zapican* now appeared alongside the Coloso. Commanded by Lt Alberto Sghirla, she had been joined in Montevideo harbour at 2000 hrs by Lt Elvirildo Viera, with orders to start out towards the burning wreck. Steam was already partly raised and the warship was soon under way for the *Tacoma*'s position. She was hoping to stop the tug convoy but arrived too late to detain *Gigante* and her barge. Langsdorff came round in his launch, however, which was made fast alongside *Zapican* and its occupants taken on board. Langsdorff explained, in French, that they were making for Buenos Aires, as the larger country 'could dispose of far greater means for any eventuality'. Langsdorff identified himself, and said he had sunk his ship because he considered it as being 'anyhow lost because of the overwhelming superiority of the enemy'. He had respected Uruguayan waters, he said, by sinking *Graf Spee* outside them. Diplomatically, he also expressed gratitude for Uruguayan courtesy during his enforced visit.[28]

Sghirla conferred with Viera and two other officers in his cabin. They concluded that as Langsdorff was 'a senior officer of the German Navy proceeding in a launch of his ship which flew the war flag, there was no reason to prevent him from proceeding in his launch in the direction he wished'. Langsdorff told the Uruguayans they could sink his launch if they wished; however, the officers replied that it would not be necessary and he could proceed freely. They parted cordially, and *Zapican* returned to Montevideo, where Sghirla reported to Vice-Admiral Schröder, Inspector General of Marine. The latter reported after midnight to the Minister of Defence, who informed the President of the release of Langsdorff. Baldomir fully approved of Sghirla's initiative.

Langsdorff's launch, three others and the *Coloso* then set sail for Buenos Aires, rendezvous being made with the *Gigante* and *Chirigueña* during the night abreast of La Plata. Two of *Graf Spee*'s boats, leaking as a result of battle damage, had to be abandoned; but they were later salvaged by the Argentines, who reconditioned them for the use of the German Naval Attaché. A fifth boat containing, among others *Graf Spee*'s Chinese laundrymen, had been hoisted aboard *Tacoma* as it was leaking too badly. The German merchantman was ordered by the warship *Uruguay* to return to Montevideo, where it was kept under guard and eventually interned as an auxiliary warship. The Uruguayans interpreted her attempt to prevent the *Graf Spee*'s crew being interned as a violation of neutrality.

His release by the Uruguayans seems to have raised Langsdorff's spirits for a while. He appears to have come on board *Coloso*, and Hebe remembered him 'talking animatedly' to maintain morale among his men.[29] The German was much impressed, and developed a high opinion of the captain. This seems in retrospect to have been displacement activity on Langsdorff's part. His real thoughts can only be guessed at. He may have already decided on his eventual fate.

As this last little drama was played out, the British cruisers, navigation lights switched on, steamed past the Whistle Buoy within four miles of the wreck of *Graf Spee*. They directed their searchlights on the wreck. The ship was ablaze from end to end and wracked by continuing explosions. Flames were, Harwood noted, reaching almost as high as the top of her slanting control tower, 'a marvellous sight – Just TOO wonderful', as he enthusiastically wrote to his wife.[30] As Washbourne later remembered, the British ships 'then turned away and resumed our various patrols. That night we relaxed and misbehaved ourselves and, for the first time, neglected our dawn action stations. And that was that.'[31]

CHAPTER NINE

The Price of Disobedience

It took until mid-morning for the vessels carrying the *Graf Spee*'s officers and men packed 'like sardines in a tin' to arrive off Buenos Aires. Rasenack remembered feeling 'dead with hunger and completely exhausted' and Gotz feeling 'abandoned'.[1] This changed when it was noticed that the quays were crowded and when boats commissioned by the German community came out with fruit, milk, bread and other food which the hungry sailors eagerly devoured 'like hungry wolves'.[2] It took time for the tugs and their occupants to be cleared by the port authorities. The Germans claimed to be shipwrecked sailors not subject to internment. The Argentineans came under the gentlest of British pressure not to comply with this. Ovey pointed out to them: 'how deplorable it would be if Argentina, who depends so much on the exports of her products to England, should be a base and resource for manning raiders and other German vessels trying to break through our contraband control'.[3]

Probably even this subtle hint was unnecessary. Argentina had no intention of going out on a limb for Nazi Germany, for whom its sympathies were very overrated, not least by the Germans. Eventually, the German ambassador, Baron von Thermann, came out by launch to announce that the Argentines had decided to allow the Germans ashore but that internment was likely. At about 15.00 hrs the tugs came alongside the quay of the Immigrants Hotel. This three-floor building could accommodate all eight hundred or so ratings in the dormitories. Officers and senior rates went to the messes in the Naval Arsenal close by.

Tuesday the 19th was taken up with formal registration of the *Graf Spee*'s crew as the Argentine cabinet met to make the final decision on internment, the cost to be borne by the German government. Langsdorff was most disappointed that his attempts to avoid this had failed and his mood was hardly helped by comments in the Argentine and Uruguayan press. He had demonstrated 'cowardice' by not going down with his ship and had taken an overly threatening attitude in the valedictory letter that he had supposedly written in Montevideo. As his men wrote their aerogrammes home to reassure worried relatives, the pressure on the poor German captain became unbearable.

Langsdorff's decision to turn a blind eye to his standing orders – consistently repeated from Berlin – not to engage Allied warships had gone dreadfully, horrifically wrong. He had lost both his ship and thirty-seven of his crew. He might have sunk a cruiser, but there were many more where *Exeter* had come from; it was not a good exchange ratio for a fifth of Germany's limited strength in 11-in. gun capital ships. He was now stuck in Argentina for the remainder of the war; but even if he escaped from internment, his welcome in Germany from Raeder would be frosty indeed. Moreover, he had lost thirty-seven young men, all killed because of his flawed decision making. He had even failed in preventing the internment of himself and his men; now, his own instinct that he should have immolated himself with *Graf Spee*, like the ship's namesake had done perforce with his flagship in 1914, was being confirmed by the local press. Langsdorff undoubtedly felt suicidal as he saw *Graf Spee* blow up. This decision could only be confirmed by all that had happened since. Perhaps his personal sacrifice could atone, at least to an extent, for the disaster he had visited on the German Navy.

In the late afternoon, Langsdorff addressed his crew by divisions in the garden of the Immigrants Hotel. Twenty years later, Hans Gotz remembered that his captain had been positive about Argentina's welcome. He assured his men that that they were in good hands with a German community who would give every assistance. Finally, he turned to the events of the weekend: 'To meet future criticism, he (Langsdorff) stated that he did not lack personal courage to make a fight even against an overwhelming enemy and to find an honourable sailor's grave but then we would have died with him. This I remembered afterwards.'[4]

These were revealing remarks. Langsdorff had made a personal, *unauthorised* decision to engage the British. He himself was willing to die in the attempt but he felt it irresponsible to force his men to share this fate. The sacrifice had to be much more personal - at which he hinted in his concluding remarks.

'A few days ago, it was your sad duty to pay the last honours to your dead comrades. Perhaps you will be called upon to undertake a similar task in the future.'[5]

Having made the dread decision, Langsdorff could relax. That evening he met with fellow officers, the Counsellor of the German Embassy and some local expatriate Germans in the senior mess in the Arsenal. He was, reportedly, 'quite at ease', even 'animated and gay as we had not seen him for a long time'. Some, however, suspected a darker side. The Counsellor reportedly told one of the officers to 'look after your captain tonight'.[6] Langsdorff had probably already asked Ascher for his pistol, under the pretext that he might need it to defend himself. The party broke up just before midnight and Langsdorff went to his room.

Leutnant Dietrich had replaced Oberleutnant Diggins as Langsdorff's Flag Lieutenant and he saw him writing at his desk in his ground floor room. Langsdorff was writing to the ambassador to set out, succinctly and clearly, the reasons for what he was about to do.

> After a long and inward struggle, I reached the grave decision to scuttle the Panzerschiff *Graf Spee* in order that she should not fall into the hands of the enemy. I am convinced that under the circumstances this decision was the only one I could make after I

had taken my ship into the trap of Montevideo. With the ammunition remaining, any attempt to break out to open and deep water was bound to fail. And yet only in deep water could I have scuttled the ship after having used all the remaining ammunition, so preventing her falling into the hands of the enemy.

Rather than expose my ship to the danger, after her fight, of falling partly or completely into enemy hands, I have decided not to fight but to destroy the equipment and sink the ship. It was clear to me that this decision might be misinterpreted, whether intentionally or unwittingly, by persons ignorant of my motives as being attributable partly or entirely to personal considerations. Therefore I decided from the beginning to bear the consequences involved in this decision. For a captain with a sense of honour cannot separate his own fate from that of his ship.

I postponed my intention as long as I was still responsible for the welfare of the crew under my command. After today's decision of the Argentine Government, I can do no more for my ship's company. Neither will I be able to take an active part in the present conflict of my country. Now I can only prove by my death that the fighting services of the Third Reich are ready to die for the honour of their flag.

I alone bear the responsibility for scuttling the Panzerschiff *Graf Spee*. I am happy to pay with my life to prevent any possible reflection on the honour of the flag. I shall meet my fate with firm faith in the cause and future of the nation and of my Führer.

I am writing this letter to Your Excellency in the quiet of the evening, after calm reflection, in order that you may be able to inform my superior officers, and to counter any public rumours if this should become necessary.[7]

After completing his letter and one to his wife and another to his parents, Langsdorff unfolded an ensign; either the one he had hauled down in *Graf Spee* two nights before, or the one the ship had flown in battle. He then took up Ascher's pistol, turned it towards his head and pulled the trigger. The shot grazed the back of his head. Langsdorff's depression must have passed the bounds of bearability. He could not even commit suicide properly! He put the gun to his forehead and fired a final, fatal shot.[8]

At 0600 hrs the following morning an orderly brought breakfast but there was no reply. Dietrich was called and he knocked twice with the same result. The door was forced and Dietrich entered the room to find the uniformed figure of Kapitän-zur-See Hans Langsdorff lying on his bed next to the last ensign flown by *Graf Spee* (its black cross fostered the legend, soon propagated by the Argentine Foreign Minister to the British ambassador, that Langsdorff had shot himself on the old Imperial Naval flag – a gift to Allied propaganda).[9] Kay was roused and went to find Dr Härting, the Second Surgeon. He said, the doctor later remembered, '"Come at once – something has happened". He led me to the Staff Officers' quarters in the same building and pointed to the room of our Captain. "It must have happened between two and four in the morning", he said. I found Captain Langsdorff with a shot through his temple and lying on our battle flag – from his right hand the revolver had almost slipped; rigor mortis had not yet set in. The bullet was to be seen stuck in the parquet floor. On a table nearby lay a letter to the German Ambassador, which I handed to the Executive Officer. Without altering anything in the position of the corpse I began my death watch at his door until the Argentine officials, already summoned, arrived.'[10]

Langsdorff was buried with full naval honours in Buenos Aires. Crowds filed by the coffin and lined the streets as the procession of the *Graf Spee*'s officers and ship's company, the German ambassador and representatives of the Argentine armed forces filed from the Arsenal to the German cemetery, the captain's last resting place. There was general mourning for an honourable and humane man. Captain Pottinger was there to represent Langsdorff's former prisoners – a remarkable tribute indeed. The price of disobedience had been paid by Langsdorff personally; yet many men owed him their lives.

Part Three
Aftermath

CHAPTER TEN

Interned

On 20 December 1939, a German-speaking 'friend' of the British Naval Attaché visited the Prefectura Maritima in Buenos Aires to glean intelligence from the internees there. He reported back that *Graf Spee*'s sailors had 'a rather haggard look, dirty in aspect and listless'. They were in shock, seeming 'rather stupid and reticent . . . unfortunate sheep' dominated by the thought that they would be spending Christmas in confinement and not back home.[1] The ship's officers billeted in the Arsenal were more optimistic, however, as they had been told by the embassy that they would be given parole to obtain posts in local firms.

Although these hopes did not last long, the lot of all *Graf Spee*'s prisoners in Argentina was far from uncomfortable.[2] The Argentineans were friendly to the sailors, who were allowed out of the Immigrants Hotel to visit local Germans. The plan was to place the officers and petty officers and 25 ratings at the naval station on the island of Martin Garcia, with other sailors in groups of a hundred or so at Florencio Varela near Buenos Aires and in locations near five other cities. The transfers took place in 1940. The men at Martin Garcia were allowed to visit Buenos Aires once every two weeks on parole. In 1944 the remaining internees were re-grouped with Martin Garcia's petty officers and ratings, others going to a disused hotel at Sierra de la Ventana in the hill country to the south of Buenos Aires province.

The remaining officers moved to Florençio Varela, which may not have been popular with the remaining internees there as the ratings at Martin Garcia had specifically asked to be separated from the officers! Despite the 'Socialism' in 'National Socialism', relations between other ranks and officers were always tricky in the Kriegsmarine.

In March 1945, Argentina belatedly declared war on Germany. But the regime for the *Graf Spee* men did not change, even though they were now officially prisoners of war. In 1946, most of the Germans were repatriated in the *Highland Monarch*, escorted, in a nice touch, by HMS *Ajax*. A few had married wives they took home but no less than 168 remained in Uruguay, where they were later joined by returning former *Graf Spee* internees, Argentina being a much more attractive prospect than postwar Germany in which to resume civilian life. Some five hundred or so former *Graf Spee* personnel, almost half the ship's complement, eventually settled in Argentina.

The officers who remained were the bare minimum required to look after the men. Kapitän Kay, the executive officer; Korvettenkapitän Hopfner, second Navigating Officer; Korvettenkapitän Nakotter, Paymaster and Chief Administrative Officer; Leutnant Drews, his deputy; Dr Peerenboom, the ship's doctor and Bandmaster Kunz. The others had felt that duty impelled them to escape. It was not too difficult to evade the Argentine police surveillance, although the latter was serious and did not make things easy. German Intelligence assisted the escapees, as did local Germans; local officials also demonstrated some sympathy. The first to go was Ascher, the gunnery officer, in January 1940. He got on board a flight and flew home via Italy. Leutnants Dietrich and Bludau next escaped in March via the southern lakes; and no less than thirteen made their escape in April when it was learned they were to be transferred to Martin Garcia. This group included Korvettenkapitäns Klepp and Wattenberg and Oberleutnant Rasenack. They got out of the Arsenal when the electrical engineer among the escapees caused a short circuit in the lighting system.

Wattenberg was hidden by a German family in Buenos Aires for four weeks and then flew to Chile in disguise. He later met up with

Dietrich and Bludau, who had walked across the Andes. Most of the escaping officers flew home via Bolivia, Brazil, and – using the transatlantic Italian air service – via the Cape Verde islands and Seville to Rome. Others, such as Rasenack, were ordered to return by sea. Rasenack now took the identity of a Bulgarian commercial traveller; but his attempt with a fellow officer to sail home through the Panama Canal led to temporary internment by the Americans. The Germans were able to persuade their captors to release them onto a Japanese ship that got them to the Pacific coast of the USA. They then crossed to Japan and eventually Korea. The two 'commercial travellers' then returned to Germany by the Trans-Siberian railway (Russia having not yet entered the war), arriving home on 1 September, 1940.

The proposed move to the island of Martin Garcia persuaded a few N.C.O.s to try escaping too. One Chief, Hans Fiber, was taken ill; and, while in hospital, befriended a German nurse, who smuggled in civilian clothes in which he escaped to a waiting car to be taken to a safe house. He was moved to Tigre Island, where he found three other *Graf Spee* escapees. Equipped with false papers, he teamed up with another Chief, Hein Wild. The pair were helped by local Germans to cross the Andes and get to Santiago in Chile, from where they eventually passed into Peru to board, disguised as Chilean businessmen, a Japanese merchantman. The ship took them to Japan and, like Rasenack, they made their way back to Berlin by train.

Escape from Martin Garcia was more difficult; but on the anniversary of the Battle of Tannenberg in September, no fewer than seventeen officers crammed into a launch to be taken to Tigre for the celebration. The British had warned the Argentines of a possible escape, but to no avail. The officers were helped by the local escape organisation to go their various ways. One, Kapitänleutnant Gunter Schiebusch, was helped by Germans to enter Brazil on a false visa via Paraguay. He took the identity of a member of Paraguay's German community, but it seems the disguise was not too effective; and it was only with the connivance of the Brazilian consul in Asunción that he was able to fly to São Paulo and, eventually, home.

Once back in Germany, the officers resumed active service. Ascher went to a real battleship, the new *Bismarck*, although not in the post of gunnery officer. He had the satisfaction of seeing HMS *Hood* blown up, some revenge at least for the loss of *Graf Spee*; but any gratification was brief. When Bismarck was sunk he was lost with her. Rasenack served in *Tirpitz* and survived the war to return to settle in Argentina, where he became President of the association founded for former *Graf Spee* sailors. Wattenberg became a highly successful U-boat commander, sinking fourteen ships with a total tonnage of 86,000 tons – rather better than his old Panzerschiff's record. His U-162 was eventually sunk in the West Indies and he spent the rest of the war as a prisoner in the USA, although he did try to escape once more, this time less successfully. Another U-boat commander was Diggins, who had been one of the officers left behind in Montevideo. He managed to escape to Buenos Aires by stowing away in the river ferry. He commanded successively U-751 and U-458 before being sunk in the latter in the Mediterranean in 1943. He survived to join the West German Federal Navy in 1957.

Also left behind in Montevideo were five prize officers of the merchant marine reserve, Herzberg, Dittman, Sorensen, Ulpts and Schunemann. They reverted to mercantile status, which meant they could be released. Sorensen married the daughter of the owner of the comfortable estancia where they had first been interned; the other four tried to return to Germany. Dittmann and Ulpts joined at Santos, respectively, the German naval auxiliary *Dresden* and the German merchant ship *Babitonga*. Also in *Dresden* was another escapee, Leutnant Herbert Fröhlich, who had been promoted from Wireless CPO by Langsdorff for his decoding and monitoring skills. *Dresden* rendezvoused with the disguised German raider *Atlantis*, which the two German officers joined. *Babitonga* also met *Atlantis*, and Ulpts found himself put in charge of some of the men from her prizes. They eventually transferred to a naval auxiliary, *Alstertor*; but, like *Babitonga* herself, this ship fell foul of the British blockade and was forced to scuttle. Ulpts became a prisoner of war. The other two returned to occupied France after *Atlantis* was sunk and her crew saved; first by an auxiliary, and then, when that was sunk, by U-boats which towed the boats to safety.

Less lucky was Herzberg, who took the trans-Siberian route. He served twice in the disguised raider *Komet* and went down with her when she was torpedoed by a British motor torpedo boat in the Channel in 1942. The German tender, *Altmark* eventually made it back to Germany, but without her 299 prisoners. She was spotted by RAF aircraft off Norway on 16 February, 1940. In a well-known and daring piece of gunboat diplomacy, the captured seamen were freed from the embittered attentions of Kapitän Dau by the destroyer HMS *Cossack* under the command of Captain Vian in Jösing Fjord. *Altmark* went aground in the incident but was repaired, renamed *Uckermark* and eventually lost in an accidental fuelling explosion at Yokohama in November 1942.

CHAPTER ELEVEN

The Victors

Harwood wanted to put into Montevideo immediately after the scuttling to reprovision *Ajax* and to send *Achilles* to Buenos Aires, but the local diplomats dissuaded him from doing so. The welcome he would receive in Montevideo might well have embarrassed the Uruguayans by its warmth and the ambassador in Rio was anxious not to be seen in any sense to be pressuring the Argentineans in their treatment of the internees. Harwood was offered visits to Punta del Este in Uruguay and Mar del Plata in Argentina, but did not wish to waste the visit he was allowed every three months in each country on these minor ports. So he sent *Achilles* to join the damaged *Exeter* in the Falklands, following on himself in *Ajax*; *Cumberland* arrived on Christmas Eve and the entire squadron spent Christmas together. *Achilles* then patrolled around the Horn area to look for *Altmark* before rejoining *Ajax* for the delayed visits that took place from 3–5 January.[1]

The reception in Montevideo was indeed as warm and enthusiastic as Millington-Drake had expected. McCall reported it to the Admiralty as 'one triumphal progress', and 'wonderfully unneutral'. The 'most striking thing' had been 'the spontaneity and extent of the welcome of the ordinary people, which could hardly have been greater had this been a British colony.' Harwood's personal popularity had 'added to the zest of the applause'.[2] He had time only for one round of golf between receptions hosted by the President (attended also by the

Vice-President, Guani, Santos and Schröder), the Anglo–Uruguayan Trade Association and other pro-Allied committees. Harwood's command of Spanish stood him in good stead on these occasions. The British Patriotic Committee presented him with a cheque for £1,000 for the dependents of those killed in the battle. Captain Daniel of the Houlder line described the welcome in the Uruguayan capital in a letter to his sister: 'If you could have seen the way the Uruguayan people welcomed the British cruiser it would have gladdened your heart. They came down in crowds, waving Union Jacks and cheering. They gave the ship a tumultuous welcome . . . absolutely triumphal'.[3] *Achilles* had a more restrained, but nevertheless, what her captain found a 'most astounding' warm welcome in Buenos Aires, being allowed to stay forty-eight hours to repair her engines.[4] Her junior rates were allowed ashore, though only in parties to prevent clashes with the German internees; but it was noted that, on occasion, British and German personnel did meet on quite amicable terms.

After this triumph, *Ajax* sailed for home and Harwood transferred his flag to *Achilles*, which was relieved in turn as flagship by the old 7.5-in. gun cruiser *Hawkins* on 29 January, 1940. As the New Zealand cruiser steamed by the new flagship, the ship's company sang '*For He's a Jolly Good Fellow*', accompanied by the ship's band. Then there were three spontaneous cheers and the Maori farewell.

Achilles arrived home in Auckland on 22 February 1940. A flotilla of small craft met her to escort her, and whistles and sirens sounded a cacophony of salute. When the ship docked, the first to board were the Governor General and Deputy Prime Minister along with other members of the Government. Cheered by crowds, the ship's company marched through decorated streets in a parade to the town hall. There, Peter Fraser, the Deputy Prime Minister, said that the *Achilles* men had exceeded any expectation that might have come from friend or foe alike. Telegrams of congratulation were read, and Captain Parry received a Maori mat and Nelson's first Midshipman's dirk, which had been acquired by the mayor of the city from the Hardy estate.[5]

The following day a similar event was held in London for the crews of the two British cruisers. *Exeter* had made good progress with repairs despite lack of facilities in the Falklands. Equipment was brought by pack horse when required. Cosmetic work was done to disguise the damage. The forward turrets were freed by having the damaged armour cut away and were put into normal fore and aft position by hydraulic jacks. Sheet tin and corrugated iron donated by proud Falklanders replaced the damaged plates. Only the after turret could be put back into action and ammunition was transferred into the after magazine to fill it in case the ship encountered the enemy on her return voyage. The topmasts were removed and other structural damage repaired as much as possible to make the ship watertight and seaworthy. Churchill, the First Lord, took a personal interest in *Exeter* and arranged strong escort home. Two County class cruisers accompanied the ship to 200 miles east of Pernambuco, where they were relieved by the capital ships that had played their phantom part in *Graf Spee*'s sinking, *Renown* and *Ark Royal*, together with two destroyers. After a stop in Freetown, *Exeter* steamed northwards to the Western Approaches, being given a heavy anti-submarine escort of no fewer than eight destroyers. These were needed, as a large merchantman was sunk within sight of the warships as they neared Plymouth, entering the sound in darkness on St Valentine's day evening.

Rumours of *Exeter*'s return to her home port swept over the city and crowds gathered on the Hoe on the morning of the 15th to see the cruiser moored a mile away. With her band playing and her ship's company lining the decks, she then moved up to the Devonport naval base, the shores of the Tamar being thronged by well-wishers. At Mount Wise stood the official welcoming party in salute, the First Lord himself, the First Sea Lord, Admiral Sir Dudley Pound, the Chancellor of the Exchequer, Sir John Simon and the C-in-C Plymouth, Admiral Dunbar-Nasmyth. The VIPs boarded the cruiser as soon as she berthed and Churchill addressed the ship's company on the quarterdeck. With his customary theatricality, he told the Exeters:

> In this sombre, dark winter, when, apart from the Navy, we have been at war and yet not at war . . . the brilliant action of the Plate, in which you played a memorable part, came like a flash of light and colour on the scene, carrying with it an encouragement to all who are fighting – to ourselves and to our allies. This great action will long be told in song and story. When you came up the river this morning, when you entered the harbour and saw the crowds cheering on the banks, one might almost think that there were other spectators in the great shades of the past, carrying us back to the days of Drake and Raleigh, to the great sea dogs of the olden times. If their spirits brooded on this scene you would be able to say to them, "We, your descendants, still make war and have not forgotten the lessons you taught."[6]

The men were then given immediate shore leave. *Ajax* had already returned in December to undergo repairs at Chatham.

It was on 23 February that the Exeters joined the Ajaxes, and six of the merchant captains kept prisoner in *Graf Spee*, in the parade in London. The 766 men marched through cheering crowds from Waterloo behind the Chatham Royal Marine band across Westminster Bridge to Horseguards Parade, where there stood a small group of relatives of those who had lost their lives in the battle. In Horseguards, the Admiralty door opened and out came the King, the Duke of Kent, Prime Minister Neville Chamberlain and other ministers, together with Churchill and the whole Board of Admiralty. It was a brilliantly staged, triumphal event. Captains Bell and Woodhouse were presented to the King, who inspected the parade and presented a posthumous Conspicuous Gallantry Medal to the widow of Marine Russell of *Exeter*, while the Queen, who had watched from a window in the Admiralty, met the bereaved relatives.

The parade then marched past the King on its way to Guildhall and a City lunch attended by 850 people, including Lady Harwood. Churchill made another speech in which he told how, in a dark winter, the victory of the Plate had 'warmed the cockles of the British heart.'[7]

On 29 February, the Exeters were hosted by their namesake city to a similar civic lunch. Captain Bell was made a freeman of the City. There is no doubt that the Battle did strike a positive cord during the frustrations of the 'phoney war' – something on which the Government naturally played for all it was worth.

****

Harwood returned home in the Autumn to become Assistant Chief of Naval Staff (Foreign), a good post for an officer with his experience. One cannot but be struck by the thoughtful and analytical nature of the papers he wrote. He clearly saw the dangers of ignoring the defence of Singapore; and suggested, without result, greater realism and clarity in Far Eastern strategy. Less fortunate was Churchill's decision to appoint Harwood to replace Admiral Andrew Cunningham as C-in-C Mediterranean at a most difficult time in May 1942. By this time, the Mediterranean campaign was being turned on its head, the desert war being fought to sustain Malta rather than Malta being a base to support the North African campaign. Harwood has been criticised for his actions in this crucible of high command, but in fairness he had to cope with an impossible and strategically illogical situation that became more favourable only when his command was split for the Operation Torch landings. He remained on station until April 1943 as C-in-C Levant, but the strains of high command broke his health and he had to haul down his flag due to heart problems. He served for about a year as Flag Officer in the Orkneys and Shetlands in 1944–5 but his health finally forced retirement in November 1945.

Harwood's abilities as a Commander-in-Chief are matters of controversy. But there can be no doubt that he was one of the finest Foreign Station cruiser Commodores in the history of the Royal Navy. Harwood combined political astuteness, diplomatic finesse, tactical skill and brilliant leadership. Langsdorff could not have faced a more difficult opponent.

As for his captains, two became Admirals. Woodhouse of *Ajax* became captain of the battleship *Howe*, received his flag and was Director of Naval Ordnance at the Admiralty. He was then sent out in 1946–7 to command the declining major units of the Pacific Fleet, finally becoming C-in-C East Indies Station until retirement in 1950. Parry of *Achilles* became professional head of the New Zealand Division of the Royal Navy as First Naval Member of the New Zealand Navy Board in 1940. He returned to command *Renown* in 1943 and was a force commander at the Normandy landings after promotion to Rear Admiral. He then served on the staff of the Allied Naval Commander of the Expeditionary force, ending up as his Berlin representative. Parry became Director of Naval Intelligence in 1946 and his final job took him back to the Commonwealth as first C-in-C of the Indian Navy from 1948 to 1951. He retired as a full Admiral.

Bell of *Exeter* was a little less lucky. He was appointed Flag Captain and Chief Staff Officer to Flag Officer Malaya and was involved in the debacle of its conquest by the Japanese. Abandoning everything, he escaped from Singapore in a yacht the day before it fell, crossing Sumatra to Java and eventually reaching Freemantle by merchant ship. Bell retuned to the Far East in command of the battleship *Anson* in 1945, but his gruelling experiences of the war caused a nervous collapse compounded by tuberculosis.[8] He therefore missed promotion and left the service on grounds of ill-health in 1947.

Oddly enough, his old ship also found her way to the Far East, but, sadly, she did not escape. *Exeter* was given a long refit that lasted for over a year. She was so badly damaged that leaving her as a hulk in the Falklands was considered; but Churchill insisted his 'hero' cruiser be brought home, repaired and returned to service. When she finally emerged in March 1941, *Exeter* had new twin 4–in. A.A. gun mountings, two new eight-barrelled pom-poms and a Type 279 radar. She went first to the Home Fleet but was then sent as emergency reinforcement to the Eastern Fleet after Japan went to war in 1942. On 27 February, she was involved in the first part of the Battle of the Java Sea in which she was hit by both a torpedo and gunfire. The torpedo failed to explode but the gunfire seriously damaged her boilers and caused her to fall out of line. After the defeat she tried to escape through the Sunda Strait; but on 1 March, ran into a powerful Japanese force of cruisers and destroyers which inflicted further shell damage on her boiler room and immobilised her. As she was being scuttled, a 24-in Long Lance torpedo fired by the Japanese destroyer *Inazuma* hastened her doom.

Ajax and *Achilles* were, as usual, more fortunate. *Ajax* was repaired and returned to fully operational condition by July 1940 when she was sent to the Mediterranean, her major area of interest for the rest of the ship's career. Shortly after arriving on station she sank two Italian destroyers and damaged a third (which was finished off by *Exeter*'s half-sister, *York*). *Ajax* took part in the battle of Matapan in Vice Admiral Pridham-Wippell's cruiser force, and in the harrowing evacuations from Greece and Crete in 1941. After Malta Convoy duty she was home to Chatham for repairs once more and a modern radar fit in the Summer of 1942. *Ajax* returned to the Mediterranean but was bombed and seriously damaged in Bone harbour on the first day of 1943. Most of the rest of the year was thus spent being repaired in New York before *Ajax* returned to the Mediterranean for Aegean operations. She was detached to cover the Normandy landings before returning to the Mediterranean for the landings in the South of France and operations in Greek waters. She provided accommodation for Churchill when the Prime Minister visited Athens in December 1944 during the suppression of the Communists there. Although *Ajax* escorted *Graf Spee*'s sailors in their journey home in *Highland Monarch* in 1946, she remained a Mediterranean Fleet cruiser until 1948. Then she returned to Chatham for the last time to pay off, being broken up at Newport the following year, a possible sale to Chile having fallen through.

Achilles was the longest-lived. She fought in the Solomon Islands in 1942–3, being damaged by bombing, and then came back from New Zealand for a major refit and modernisation at Portsmouth, which involved increasing her A.A. armament, fitting a comprehensive radar kit and adding fighter direction capability. To provide the necessary weight and space she lost one of her after 6-in. turrets, which had in any case been damaged in action. This new tactical balance stood her in good stead when she returned to what was now the Royal New Zealand Navy for service with the British Pacific Fleet. She was returned by the New Zealanders in 1946 and placed in reserve. In 1948 she was considered suitable to become the first major unit of the new Indian Navy, a force led by her old commanding officer of 1939, Admiral Parry. Renamed *Delhi*, she had a long life with her new owners, only being paid off for scrap in 1978. One high spot of her Indian career was playing herself in the film *Battle of the River Plate*, shot in the Mediterranean off Malta and premiered in 1956. The New Zealanders considered preservation, but towing the ship from India was itself prohibitively expensive. Instead, various parts of the ship, notably a turret and a director, were returned to Auckland. The latter stands today in the museum at the Royal New Zealand Navy's Devonport naval base.

Another ship that played herself in the film was HMS *Cumberland*. She returned from the South Atlantic Station in 1941 and spent most of the rest of the war with the Home Fleet, covering Arctic convoys during 1942–3. After service in the Far East and a period in reserve, she was converted to a gunnery trials cruiser from 1949 to 1951, in which role she lasted until 1959. The conversion involved the removal of her original armament, which makes the cheers meeting her arrival 'off Montevideo' in the film seem a little strange to the sharp-eyed observer, who might note her conspicuous lack of guns! *Cumberland* did important work in her last rôle, playing a notable part in the development of the fully automatic, rapid-fire 6-in. guns fitted to *Tiger*, *Blake* and *Lion*, the Royal Navy's last gun-armed cruisers.

CHAPTER TWELVE

Spee: the final battle

And *Graf Spee*? The wreck burned for four days and nights, then lay there, tempting the British mightily to find out what remained of its secrets. The initial point of interest was her radar. McCall had interviewed some of the *Graf Spee*'s crew, who remarked that the rangefinder would often be seen revolving at sea. Photographs taken of the ship before and after scuttling, including a picture passed on by a friendly chemist developing a film for one of *Graf Spee*'s officers, were studied, and it was concluded that the dismountable antenna did indicate some form of high-frequency radio equipment, probably radar, which the British were themselves developing. McCall was told to make a careful examination of the wreck with a view to finding out more about the mysterious aerial. To assist him, he was sent the exotically-named Lebouchère H. Bainbridge-Bell, an Air Ministry scientific officer and a member of Britain's original radar development team. He had come via Paris, where the Deuxième Bureau had shown him more pictures of *Graf Spee*, and then by air to Rio from Marseilles. The flying boat service did not normally carry passengers in wartime but an exception was made in the circumstances. He arrived in Montevideo on 7 February.[1]

Meanwhile, the somewhat shady but 'energetic' manager of a local import–export firm, Julio Vega-Helguara, approached Millington-Drake. He was known for his contacts with the Secretary General of the Ministry for Foreign Affairs, and Langmann had approached him to use his influence to obtain official diplomatic recognition for the wireless monitoring specialists from *Graf Spee*. Apparently, the Germans hoped to use them to set up an interception station on the east coast of South America. Vega was unable to obtain visas for the Germans from the Uruguayans, but on his own initiative suggested a possible purchase of the wreck for the scrap. Vega probably already thought he could interest the British in rather more than scrap metal. He told his friend Millington-Drake of Langmann's approach and the British Minister telegraphed to London on 15 January, asking if there was indeed any interest from the Admiralty in obtaining the wreck. The latter replied to the Foreign Office on 29 January expressing mild interest, and asking for Millington-Drake to pursue the matter further. The interest in the radar seems not at this stage to have communicated itself to the Admiralty in general, to the extent of there being any great enthusiasm for purchase.

To keep his intermediary with the Uruguayan Foreign Ministry sweet, Langmann expressed a willingness to sell. The original plan was that the Germans would sell the ship to Vega for the equivalent of £3,000 with half-shares in any scrap proceeds. Vega asked Millington-Drake if the British might lend him the money, plus a subsidy to recover the scrap. This would, as one Admiralty official pointed out, effectively be a licence fee to examine the wreck. Some kind of payment would indeed be necessary. McCall told London on 12 February that the difficulties of obtaining a clandestine examination with his recently arrived expert were 'insurmountable'. The Uruguayans had been keeping strict watch on the wreck since some sailors from the cruiser USS *Quincy* had swum out to it on a recent visit. On 17 February, Millington-Drake, who had himself persuaded friends to swim out to the wreck and take photographs, informed London that the Uruguayan authorities were not now allowing anyone within two hundred yards of the wreck without a permit.

Vega's proposal offered a way out of this problem. Arrangements for the sale had been progressing. Together with Voulminot (his chosen contractor), two German officers and Kirkpatrick, a local expatriate businessman, he had spent three hours on the wreck on the 16th. It was in much better condition than previously thought; and, in a telegram, Millington-Drake suggested that Vega, using his influence with the Germans, could purchase the wreck outright for £7,500 to £15,000. Lt Cdr Johnston, the Staff Officer (Intelligence) in Montevideo, in a separate signal to the Director of Naval Intelligence, stressed the value of the information to be gained – especially the nature of the mysterious 'wireless grid.'

Enthusiasm had already been expressed in certain quarters in the Admiralty for the original purchase. The new plans, which reflected the increased information value of the wreck, and which took the Germans out of the loop completely, met with even greater favour. On 20 February, Millington-Drake was authorised to subsidise Vega up to £20,000. Vega, who told Millington-Drake he was acting on behalf of Britain with no thought of profit, suggested £10,000 in the first instance; Langmann asked for £20,000. Eventually on the 23rd they settled on £14,000, after Vega had bribed the President of the German Chamber of Commerce to the tune of £200. Letters had been exchanged and the Uruguayan government had no objection. The purchase was outright and unconditional in Vega's name. The British Admiralty were the secret owners, but they were careful not to accept responsibility for the wreck in the agreement drawn up with Vega.

The day after the purchase was concluded, Johnston reported to London that a party from the Uruguayan Inspectorate General of Marine, who had already taken significant amounts of equipment from *Graf Spee* to the Arsenal in Montevideo, had made an attempt to blow up the *Graf Spee*'s tower mainmast. This was done without reference to any other part of the Uruguayan government and the British, some of whom suspected Vice Admiral Gostavo Schröder, the Inspector General of Marine, of the pro-German sympathies his name suggested, thought this had been done at German behest. The charge, however, failed to explode. On the 27th, an anonymous caller with a German accent threatened the British embassy with another attempt, and the atmosphere was reported as 'tense'. Vega duly put a guard around the wreck and obtained the support of the Navy to put a naval guard on board. He formally took possession on 1 March 1940.

A vital part of the cover story was that Vega intended to sell *Graf Spee*'s steel to British and Italian firms; this would allow British 'scrap dealers' openly to visit the wreck. Langmann seems to have been willing to go along with this as he wished to keep Vega sweet for his own purposes. The Uruguayan Government also found it a convenient story. Finally, as a 'representative' of Thos. Ward Ltd of Sheffield, Bainbridge-Bell got on board *Graf Spee* on 6 March at low water to climb the mast and inspect the radio room at its peak, together with the associated 'wireless grid'. After a second visit on the 7th, he had enough evidence from the antenna and a cathode ray tube indicator to signal to London that *Graf Spee* had been fitted with a radar operating at about 57 cm. As samples to take back to Britain he took parts of the antenna and the cathode ray tube. The parts are now preserved at HMS *Collingwood*. He made a third visit before returning home with, as Millington-Drake put it to London on the 10th, his 'well-worthwhile results'. As the Admiralty wrote to the Treasury in 1941, when the latter complained about their £14,000 that had 'gone down the drain': 'The examination of the *Graf Spee* (by Bainbridge-Bell) was most valuable in establishing the use of R.D.F. by the enemy. It also provided sufficient technical detail in this matter to guide us in the search for enemy R.D.F. in general and in the revising and preparation of equipment and countermeasures.'[2]

It had been thought necessary to have a real representative of Ward's to appear in Uruguay to give the cover story some credibility. A civilian, Mr Frederick A. Smith was chosen to fly out as quickly as possible and the French were persuaded to give him another place on their flying boat from Marseilles. Air travel in the war years was an uncomfortable and unusual business and it proved too much for Smith. He arrived in Buenos Aires seriously ill and an emergency operation did not save him. He died on 6 March, the final casualty of the battle of the River Plate.

****

Three days following the death of Smith, Lt Guy Kilroy, an ordnance expert from the Admiralty's torpedo establishment at HMS *Vernon*, Portsmouth, and Mr Ken Purvis from the Directorate of Naval Construction, took ship in the ill-fated Cunarder *Lancastria* to New York. On arrival, they travelled by train to Miami for onward transit by air to Rio and finally to Montevideo. Vega had by now taken a large number of photographs of the *Graf Spee* which caused a list to be produced of items of interest: rangefinders and fire control equipment, radios and radio direction finding equipment, conning tower and bridge instruments, torpedoes and tubes, aircraft catapult, turret, hull material and construction details, degaussing equipment and armour, together with evidence of the effects of British shells. Kilroy and Purvis were to obtain this information as purported representatives of Ward's. Unfortunately, their cover was compromised by sloppy work in their passports and visas and a highly anxious Millington-Drake insisted that new documents be issued in Rio.

Kilroy and Purvis made their first visit to the wreck on 1 April and returned with what Millington-Drake described as 'much valuable information'. They were soon joined by Smith's replacement as representative of Ward's, Mr Stanley J. Dyal, who seems to have taken charge of the trio. After more examination of the wreck, Dyal reported back on 9 April that all *Graf Spee*'s decks were underwater and only her superstructure was showing There was about 1,000 tons of scrap above the waterline and some of the 5.9-in. and 4.1-in. guns could be salvaged. The heavy explosions aft and amidships prevented any hope of salvage of the ship itself. Damage to the hull and decks was beyond repair. The forward scuttling charge was also still suspended under water and this could go off at any time. The ship had gone further down into the mud by about eight to ten feet since scuttling and was probably sinking all the time. It might be feasible, Dyal reported, to lift her bodily, but the plant was not available and the cost would be 'fantastic'. The value of the scrap recovered would not pay for such an operation; and Dyal doubted if it was even worthwhile financially to take the scrap above the waterline.

Dyal had the previous day (the 8th) met Millington-Drake, Harwood and McCall and told them of the situation. It was agreed that there should be a further meeting that evening, involving himself, Millington-Drake, Kilroy, Purvis, Vega, Johnston and two British businessmen who had been helpful so far – Maclean (who had already received £1,000 for his services) and Walsh. They agreed that raising the vessel was impossible; but that an attempt to recover expenditure and glean intelligence might be made by recovering the torpedo warhead, one or more 11-in. guns with their shells and other materials including armour plate. Divers were planned to inspect the wreck on the 10th. The local ship repair firm of Ragusci and Voulminot were apparently interested in buying the wreck off Vega, as they had hopes of raising her and reconditioning and selling the diesel engines.

This further examination led to a detailed list of items to be recovered from *Graf Spee* being forwarded to London on 12 April. It included armour plate from the forward turret and conning tower, one each of the port 37-mm and 4.1-in. mountings, a stabilised director control tower with base, a port 5.9-in. gun complete with mounting, one or more of the forward three 11-in. guns and examples of welding, plates and instruments. Export of scrap metal was not normally allowed by the Uruguayan authorities, but Vega would call it 'material in transit'. Dyal warned that the cost of getting the material ashore would be high, some £3–4,000, Ragusci and Voulminot being the contractors. The latter firm naturally insisted that the explosives in the turret be rendered safe and this seems to have been done, either by the Germans, hired by Voulminots for the purpose, or by Kilroy using Davis apparatus requisitioned to dive on the wreck.

The weather now intervened. A serious storm blew up on 14–16 April, which caused the remains of *Graf Spee* to heel over to an angle of fifty degrees. This and further damage to the ship made the removal of many of the desired items impossible. All that could be removed, once the explosives had been rendered safe, were a 4.1-in. stabilised mounting, the searchlight, a prismatic periscope, dampers and anchorage from the aloft control position, motors from a high-angle bearing and elevation receiver instrument, a gas-proof voicepipe, and those samples of protective plating, welds and non-ferrous metals that were still accessable and useful. The British also got their hands on damage control documents 'from a certain source' on the pretext of needing details of the turrets to remove the explosives. The documents were copied and sent to London.

Their work complete, Dyal and Purvis left for home on 2 May. On the 11th, Voulminots delivered the twin 4.1-in. gun mounting and 25 tons of other material in fourteen packages to the Furness Houlder ship *Princesa* which sailed home in Freetown convoy SL34. The *Graf Spee* parts were looked after by Lt Kilroy, who arrived at Milford Haven with them on 15 June. The Naval Constructors and Ordnance experts were happy with their haul of material and information, as they too made clear in their answers to the 1941 Treasury complaint referred to above.

The range finder tower fell into the sea about two months after the British team had left, and the rest of the *Graf Spee* wreck slowly slipped beneath the waves as the elements took their toll and she sank lower and lower into the mud. In 1942, a syndicate of Greek divers led by a Mr Kalemanis requested to be allowed to take metal from the Spee with 30 per cent of the proceeds going to the British government. The scrap was to be landed at Voulminot's yard and disposed of with British permission after examination by the Americans on behalf of the British. Nothing seems to have come of this proposal.[3]

By 1948, only the remains of the foretop were visible and these had gone by 1950. *Graf Spee* had finally sunk – although a barge was damaged when it tried to sail across the wreck site in 1953. The ship, once the pride of the German navy, still lies there, submerged 4 miles and 117 yards off Montevideo. As late as 1996, a British team helped by Uruguayan navy divers removed a 5.9-in. gun, but the muddy conditions make further diving difficult. It is impossible to see anything. As one of the divers put it, 'For us, the *Graf Spee* is over.'[4]

****

As for the other Panzerschiffe, reclassified more correctly from February 1940 as heavy cruisers, it cannot be said that they proved any more effective. The Treaty of Versailles had worked, and it proved difficult to integrate these hybrids with more normal ships. They were long-range, but relatively slow compared with the latest steam ships. *Deutschland*, the first of the three, was also plain unlucky.

Hitler was worried that a ship called *Deutschland* might be sunk, handing the Allies a propaganda opportunity on a plate; and, even before *Graf Spee* had met her fate, her elder half-sister had been renamed *Lützow*, the name originally allocated to a more normal Hipper class cruiser being transferred to the USSR under the Nazi-Soviet pact. The renamed and reclassified former Panzerschiff was torpedoed by the submarine *Spearfish* during the invasion of Norway and was heavily damaged with her stern hanging off. She was out of service until 1941 when she was torpedoed again, this time by a Coastal Command Beaufort as she tried to break out into the Atlantic supported by the former *Altmark*. This meant another six months in dockyard hands. She then went north to join the battle group based in Norway. Her ill-luck continued when she ran aground at the start of the operation planned against Convoy PQ17. Repairs prevented her return to Norway until the end of 1942. She then took part in her one major sea action, the battle of the Barents Sea, when the destroyer escort of convoy JW51B held off both her and the cruiser *Hipper*. An incensed Führer then ordered the scrapping of the surface fleet, an act which caused Raeder to resign.

Thanks to the advocacy of Raeder's replacement, Admiral Dönitz, most of the German surface ships remained in service, albeit some with reduced complements. Plans for offensive operations in 1943 proved abortive, and *Lutzow* went back to the Baltic as a training ship.

In 1944 she was pressed into action once more, bombarding the advancing Soviet land forces; perhaps the most effective operations in her career, and in the theatre for which she had been originally conceived. The following year she was sunk in shallow water at Swinemunde by near-misses from RAF Lancasters carrying 12,000-lb bombs, but she continued to operate as a static battery until her ammunition was expended. In shades of events off Montevideo four and a half years before, her ship's company wrecked her before abandoning her as a burned-out hulk. In 1947 she was raised by the Soviet occupiers, who thought she might be refitted for service but she was too far gone and was scrapped.

Admiral Scheer was a little more fortunate. She did make a successful raiding cruise in 1940–1, in which she sent to the bottom the only warship ever sunk by the class, the armed merchant cruiser HMS *Jervis Bay*, in an attack on convoy HX84. This was the kind of thing Langsdorff had had in mind the previous December. *Scheer* was at large for five months in both the North and South Atlantic and the Indian Ocean, and obtained a score about twice that of *Graf Spee*, seventeen ships totalling 113,233 G.R.T.. It was the Pazerschiffe's finest hour. A planned breakout with *Tirpitz* into the Atlantic in November 1941 was cancelled by Hitler because of a supposed threat to Norway. This prevented a clash with American battleships; the U.S.A.'s quasi-war with Germany had by now escalated to the extent of U.S. warships guarding the Denmark Strait.

Transferred herself to Norway, *Admiral Scheer* took part in offensive operations, notably the sortie that resulted in the scattering of convoy PQ17; but her major direct gunnery success was limited to sinking a Soviet ice breaker in the Kara Sea. *Scheer* then returned to Germany for refit and further service in the training role. She too went into action against the advancing Red Army, but returned in 1945 for a refit at Kiel, where she was hit by five bombs on the night of 9–10 April 1945 and capsized. Parts of the hull were salvaged for scrap and the rest covered up when the site was filled in and flattened. At least she had not been scuttled.

CHAPTER THIRTEEN

The Reckoning

Their Lordships desire to express to the Captains, Officers and Ships' Companies of HMS Ajax, *HMS* Achilles *and HMS* Exeter *their high appreciation of the spirited and determined manner in which the action against the German armoured ship* Admiral Graf Spee *was conducted.*[1]

So the Admiralty signalled to Harwood's victorious ships the day *Graf Spee* was scuttled. The Battle of the River Plate was the first British victory of the Second World War and, as such, it has acquired epic proportions. It was the subject of a classic British war film premiered in front of the Queen on 29 October 1956. This was filmed off Malta using real ships rather than models; the rather larger 6-in. cruiser HMS *Sheffield* 'played' *Ajax*, a 6-in. cruiser of about the same size, HMS *Jamaica*, played *Exeter* and *Achilles* (by the 1950s, the Indian *Delhi*) and *Cumberland* (by then a gunnery trials ship) played themselves. 'Starring' as 'tiger of the sea' *Graf Spee*, was the US heavy cruiser *Salem*, one of the largest of her type ever built and a much larger and more imposing ship than *Graf Spee* had ever been. This helped confirm the legend of the power of the pocket battleship, 'one of the most formidable ships afloat', as Time magazine wrote in their review of the film. In fact, as we have seen, the *Graf Spee* and her sisters were not the most satisfactory or powerful of warships and their main weaknesses, restricted main armament and cruiser-style protection without the superior speed that might allow them to outmanœuvre and keep at arm's length vessels that might inflict significant damage upon them, were serious defects that could be exploited by a highly skilled opponent such as 'Bobby' Harwood. The essence of naval genius is calculated risk-taking; the combination of cool bravery with shrewd and rational analysis of one's opponents' weaknesses. This was the essence of Nelson's genius – and it was a quality shared by Harwood.

Harwood handled his ships as well as anyone might have expected. He presented *Graf Spee* with the two targets with which he knew she would have most difficulty in dealing and thus did much to neutralise the effectiveness of her main armament right from the start. Langsdorff can be criticised for throwing away major advantages of his heavier guns in his attempt to close to decisive range. Captain Woodhouse, however, disagreed:

> As regards the suggestion that *Graf Spee* could have gained the advantage by engaging us in retreat, i.e. for as long as possible outside our maximum gun range, it must be appreciated that *Exeter*'s maximum range was 15.5 land miles, only 3,000 yards less than that of *Graf Spee*; so that she could, with a five-knot superiority of speed and steering straight for her enemy, have got through the gap in 7.5 minutes if *Graf Spee* steered a course to enable her to use both her turrets. It is unlikely that *Graf Spee* could have fired as much as 40 rounds in this time. During the action she got one hit per 40 rounds at much easier ranges between 21,000 and 8,000 yards. I think that if she had opened fire at her maximum range, it would have been heavy odds against her getting any hit at all on Exeter, whose beam was only 58 feet, before the latter had got into the 15.5 land miles range at which she would have been able to open fire herself.[2]

Normally German ships were known for their accurate shooting; but *Graf Spee*'s shooting was far from good. That of her secondary armament was decidedly poor, with no hits from some 377 H.E. shells expended. Given the pressures the gun crews were under in their open shield mounts, coupled with action damage to hoists and fire control equipment, that is not perhaps too surprising. Moreover, there were only four guns each side. That was not much of a broadside to increase the chances of hitting by sheer weight of fire. No hits were scored from the 80 4.1-in. shells fired by the A.A. guns, again perhaps none too surprising given the action damage to the mountings and their fire control.

As for the 11-in. main armament, its performance, except at the outset of the action, was disappointing. The six guns had scored seven hits and a damaging near-miss on *Exeter*, one hit and a glancing blow on *Ajax* and a damaging near-miss on *Achilles*. This was better shooting than the British (see below) but it was not a very good return, some 2.7 per cent, on some 414 rounds fired: 200 nose-fused H.E., 184 bottom-fused H.E. and 30 armour-piercing.[3] *Graf Spee*'s gunnery officers put this down to Langsdorff's torpedo officer's tendency to over-zigzag, coupled with his orders to shift target before decisive results could be obtained. Instead of finishing off *Exeter,* he was twice distracted by the threat of the light cruisers into engaging them instead. Langsdorff's wounds did not help his tactical judgment – but the loss of the main fire control position to splinter and cable damage can have done little to aid the accuracy of the firing that took place, especially as the battle progressed. It is clear from the Germans' track chart that their impression of British movements became increasingly erroneous. The *Graf Spee*'s ability to hit hard in the vital opening minutes when her fire control was fresh and accurate (stereoscopic rangefinding always went off in action because of the psychological pressure on the range takers) was also mitigated by the malfunction in her fore turret at the worst possible moment. She had to hit hard and quickly but was in no position to do so with full effectiveness. The fore turret also gave more trouble later.

As for British gunnery, the closer ranges chosen by Langsdorff allowed for remarkably effective results from the hits that were scored with the relatively light shells. British fire, although less accurate, was rapid enough to inflict enough damage to demoralise the Germans, and sufficient to disable them, so that they were forced into the trap of a neutral harbour. *Exeter* fired about 200 shells and scored three hits, (1.5 per cent), a creditable effort considering the ship's damage. The light cruisers together fired 2,064 rounds: 809 C.P.B.C. and 14 H.E. from *Ajax* and 1,235 C.P.B.C., 5 H.E. and one solid practice round from *Achilles*.[4] These scored about twenty hits, a rate of only about one per cent. The problems of finding and keeping an accurate fire control solution on a twisting and turning smoking object travelling at nearly thirty miles an hour at a distance of several miles, and which is firing highly lethal projectiles that you can see coming in your direction, should not be underestimated. At times, the British ships lost the target and their firing became confused but such is the inevitable fog of war. As well as inflicting significant damage, the rain of British shells certainly disconcerted the wounded Langsdorff standing in his dangerously open position in the foretop. These were not the circumstances for cool judgment.

Nevertheless it is hard to see what Langsdorff could have done but taken refuge in a nearby neutral port. The damage he had suffered had to be repaired before he started a long voyage home across the equator and into the North Atlantic. His main guns had proved unreliable and his fighting capacity had been reduced very significantly with the knocking out of his main fire control position. The limited number of shells remaining was also a major problem. On the basis of the proportion of hits in the action of the 13th, he had precisely five potential hits left between the 170 A.P. and 16 base-fused H.E. shells left in his 11-in. magazines. This was not much against three cruisers, never mind the capital ships he thought the British had brought up. His reduced speed of 17 knots would also put him at a disadvantage to the much faster British ships.

Much has been made of the decision to enter 'pro-British' Montevideo rather than 'pro-German' Buenos Aires, but in fact it made little difference to *Graf Spee*'s ultimate fate. The Uruguayans did not in the event defer to British wishes, which were that *Graf Spee* should stay as long as possible until *Renown* and *Ark Royal* appeared to seal her fate. Their insistence that *Graf Spee* should sail on 17

December, although deeply distasteful to the Germans, was more against British interests than it was against theirs. If Buenos Aires had been willing to grant longer in an Argentinean port than the Uruguayans were in theirs the perceived choice for Langsdorff would have been the same – with the important difference that six *real* 15-in. guns would have been facing him at the mouth of the Plate.

It is also far from certain that Langdsdorff would have got much more of a favourable welcome in Buenos Aires than he got in Montevideo. Sir Edmond Ovey reported that Cantilo, the Argentine Foreign Minister, had always been 'very courteous and friendly in communicating any points of interest that may have been brought to his notice that he thinks might be of value to the Allied cause.' After the battle, he had congratulated Ovey on Britain's 'splendid victory' and had said that 'the only thing that really matters is that you should win the war.'[5] There was a more substantial German community in Argentina than in Montevideo to exert pressure on the government; but the record of Buenos Aires in interning the *Graf Spee*'s crew gives little evidence that they would have been any more or less neutral in any substantive way than the Uruguayans. Indeed, the local British diplomats were convinced that the two countries colluded in matter, the disposal of the crew being much easier in the larger state.

The fundamental point was that Raeder had been right and Langsdorff dreadfully and tragically wrong. The risks of a German raider engaging even inferior forces were such that they could only to be accepted in special circumstances, for instance with a convoy actually in sight – and, perhaps, not even then. Too many things could go wrong. To fight was to seal one's doom, especially so far away from home. One may sympathise with the brave and attractive German captain wishing to repeat the emblematic success of his ship's namesake in similar waters in this new war, but he was asking for the trouble he got. It is to his everlasting credit that he decided to pay with his own life, rather than that of his ship's company, the price of that fateful disobedience.

A few hours before he took his own life, Langsdorff mused on the significance and lessons of the battle in conversation with an Argentine officer, Cdr Edwardo Anmann:

> Finally and at the end, Captain Langsdorff said to me that he was convinced that the action of December 13th would be the most important action of the present war; also that the experience he gained in the present cruise convinced him that Germany should abandon that method of warfare on commerce and instead dedicate all effort to submarine war and blockade by mines, because the risks to which a ship such as the Admiral *Graf Spee* was exposed in a war against commerce were too great; for it should be borne in mind that any damage could threaten the very existence of the ship undertaking such a campaign, without having any base for support and supplies.

One German officer and 35 men had been killed in action and 60 wounded.[6] The casualties were worse on the British side. *Exeter* lost five officers and 57 ratings in the battering she received. *Ajax* and *Achilles*, less heavily hit, got off much more lightly, seven ratings being killed in the flagship and four in *Achilles*. The victors were showered with honours, all well-earned. The executive officers of each of the cruisers were awarded Distinguished Service Orders and an extra DSO went to each ship: Lt Richard De'Ath, Royal Marines, who was in charge of 'X'-turret in *Ajax* for his work in containing the damage caused by the 11-in. hit; Washbourne in *Achilles* for maintaining his fire control position after the serious splinter damage, and Commander Charles Sims, Engineering Officer of *Exeter*, who inspired his department to keep the stricken cruiser's engines running at full speed. The Distinguished Service Cross was awarded to seven officers in *Exeter* (one to Midshipman Cameron, who threw ammunition in danger of explosion over the side), six in *Ajax* (including Dreyer and Lewin) and four in *Achilles*. Distinguished Service Medals went to seventeen ratings in *Exeter*, fourteen in *Ajax* (with an extra British Empire Medal for an R.A.F. corporal serving with the ship's flight) and fourteen in *Achilles*.[7]

There was some debate as to what the battle should be called. The Uruguayans called it the Battle of Punta del Este, but there were signs that the Admiralty preferred the Battle of Lobos Island. Millington-Drake asked that this be reconsidered as it would translate as 'The Battle of the Sea Lions'! He suggested instead that 'Battle of the River Plate' be used if it did not alienate the Uruguayans and Argentines who claimed sovereignty over the estuary.[8] Churchill had less regard for Latin American sensibilities and popularised the name. It was consecrated by Dudley Pope's book and the feature film *Battle of the River Plate*. The shorter version, 'The Plate' had a brief vogue but sounded odd and fell out of use, although Millington-Drake used it in the title of his 1964 book. It might have had a slightly longer life in one form: 'The Plate' name plates were cast for the first of a new class of Southern Railway steam locomotives to be named after Allied victories. Sadly these were too few and far between in 1940, and policy changed to naming the Merchant Navy-class locomotives after shipping lines.

The effect of the River Plate victory on world opinion at the time was very positive. Naturally, Latin America was particularly impressed. Ovey in Buenos Aires reported on the effects of 'one of the most remarkable achievements in the annals of the British Navy'. There was one potential negative effect, namely the elimination of 'one of these much-vaunted pocket battleships by an inferior force and the consequent disappearance of the glamour and prestige which has surrounded this class of ship, has produced an unconscious conviction that Germany is definitely the underdog'. However, the demonstration of the implacable force of the Royal Navy had made it seem as if it was the beginning of the end for the Germans. The South American countries quietly made it clear to the British that they were unwilling to be led by the U.S.A. into an overly aggressive, anti-British interpretation of the Pan-American neutrality zone.[9]

The River Plate was a notable success for the Royal Navy. It vindicated much inter-war naval policy and was a great contrast to the events of 1914. The First Sea Lord, Admiral Sir Dudley Pound, wrote to Harwood that his action had 'set a standard for this war, a matter of great importance'.[10] Pound went on to claim that it showed how wrong had been the Troubridge court martial, when the latter had been exonerated for his failure to engage the battlecruiser *Goeben* with weaker armoured cruisers in 1914. As Harwood wrote, 'the implication is that the standard set for the last war was upset by attacking under similar conditions and getting away with it'. Pound had said that if all Harwood's ships had been sunk he would still have been right. The latter mused on what might have happened if Troubridge had pursued a similar aggressive policy without fear of loss: 'If Troubridge had acted as I did, the *Goeben* would not have got to the Dardanelles, Turkey would probably have not come in on the German side and possibly the war would have ended sooner', without the Russian Revolution.

Harwood would never have been so disloyal as to make these criticisms of Troubridge in public; but each chain in the link of history was a vital one.[11] He might have added that Craddock had engaged von Spee's squadron later in 1914 because he did not want to be subjected to the same criticism as Troubridge; and that the resulting German battle honour of Coronel had acted as a powerful influence on Langsdorff. Chains of history indeed!

In 1914, a Royal Navy with no combat experience of the latest revolutionary weapons and dominated by materiel specialists had been led by technological logic to take a cautious tactical approach, the weakness of which had become all-too apparent.[12] The inter-war navy had adopted a self-consciously different doctrine and the new system had worked against a threat for which it had been designed. A successful surface raider had been brought to book and eliminated by the application of aggressive flexibility. Perhaps, however, it was more the end of an era than a new beginning. The increasingly three-dimensional nature of naval warfare would probe the weaknesses of the Royal Navy much more effectively than *Graf Spee* had done. It was to be a long and bitter war, but the tradition of excellence to which Harwood's great and famous success had further contributed would help considerably in carrying the Royal Navy through it.

Notes

Chapter 1

1. The account of the genesis and pre-war careers of the Panzerschiffe is based on S. Breyer, *Battleships and Battlecruisers 1905–1970* (MacDonald and Janes, London, 1973); *M.J. Whitley, German Capital Ships of World War Two* (Arms and Armour, London, 1989) and W. Rahn 'German Naval Strategy and Armament During the Interwar Period' in P. O'Brien (Ed.) *Fighting the Next War at Sea; Technology, Shipbuilding and Future Combat in the Twentieth Century and Beyond* (Frank Cass, London, forthcoming).
2. Whitley, *Op Cit*, insists that *Graf Spee* had a uniform 100-mm belt but admits that her armour records have not survived. A later German source that is aware of Whitley's work, P*anzerschiffe der Deutschland-Klasse* (Bernard und Graefe, Bonn, 1993) includes a detailed table upon which this section is primarily based. G. Bidlingmeir, '*K.M. Admiral Graf Spee*', in *Warships in Profile, Vol. 1* (Profile Publications, Windsor, n.d.), an excellent short source on the ship and the battle, also gives the lower figures.
3. Armament details primarily from John Campbell, *Naval Weapons of World War Two* (Conway, London, 1985).
4. All German sources insist on this point.
5. Whitley, *Op Cit*, pp. 22–3.
6. For ship details, see Conway's *All the World's Fighting Ships 1906–1921*, and *1922–1946* (Conway Maritime Press, London, 1985 and 1980).
7. Ibid., pp. 29–30.
8. D. Howse, *Radar at Sea* (Macmillan, London, 1993) pp. 45–49; E. Millington-Drake, *The Drama of Graf Spee and the Battle of the River Plate: A Documentary Anthology* (hereafter: Millington-Drake, *Drama*) (Peter Davis, London, 1964), pp. 81 and 183.
9. Millington-Drake, *Drama*, p. 82.

Chapter 2

1. *Graf Spee 1939, The German Story* is based on captured German records.

Copy in the Harwood papers; also in the Parry papers in the Imperial War Museum, London (I.W.M.).

2. Bidlingmeir *Op. Cit.*
3. Details of voyage unless otherwise noted from *The German Story* and Millington-Drake, *Drama*.
4. Intelligence report based on interviews with merchant ships' captains. Public Record Office (P.R.O., London) ADM 223/69.
5. *Ibid.*
6. Letter from Admiral Kranke to Millington-Drake, Millington-Drake Collection, I.W.M. London, Box 24.
7. Translation in P.R.O. London, ADM 223/25.
8. *The German Story*, p. 3.
9. *Ibid.*, pp. 4–5.
10. *Führer Conferences on Naval Affairs 1939*, produced by the Admiralty, August 1947, pp. 45–9. Copy in the Harwood papers.
11. *Führer Conferences*, pp. 18–19.
12. *The German Story*, p. 6.
13. *Ibid.*
14. Photostat excerpt from Langsdorff's war diary, Millington-Drake Collection, Box 24.
15. P. Dove, *I was the Graf Spee's Prisoner* (Cherry Tree Books, 1940).

Chapter 3

1. Dove, *ibid.*
2. F.W. Rasenack, *Panzerschiff Graf Spee* (as translated by Millington-Drake in *Drama*, p. 134).
3. This section is from a photostat of the war diary in the Millington-Drake Collection at the I.W.M., London, Box 24. Due to its importance I have had it re-translated by Andrea Elner. It is also summarised on pp. 10–11 of *The German Story.*
4. *Ibid.*
5. See Note 2.
6. As reported by Wattenberg, quoted in Millington-Drake, *Drama*, p. 174. According to Bidlingmeir, *Op Cit.* p. 88, Langsdorff went so far as to say the contacts would provide 'some fine target practice'.
7. Wattenberg, *ibid.*

Chapter 4

1. Unless otherwise stated, the primary sources for this chapter are Millington-Drake, *Drama* and Chapter 2 of G. Bennett, *Battle of the River Plate* (Ian Allan, London, 1972).
2. Admiralty telegram quoted in *Drama*, p. 102.
3. Appendix 5, Bennett, *Op. Cit.*, pp. 66–7.
4. There is a description of this in Millington-Drake's correspondence with Robert Oldfield, a member of *Ajax*'s ship's company, in Box 22 of the Millington-Drake Collection at the I.W.M.
5. The message pad 'doodle' is a famous document. Harwood set great store by it and had several copies made by an expert forger, hence the number of apparent 'originals'. The true original is still with the Harwood family, who also provided a memorandum on the World's Fair visit, based on the memory of Lady Joan Harwood.

6. Harwood's report of 30 December 1939 was printed as part of the Admiralty's battle summary, *The River Plate Battle.* This will be cited as Harwood, by paragraph number; this is para. 3.
7. Explained in a letter from Captain R.C. Medley to the Director-General, Imperial War Museum, 3 September 1953; copy in Harwood papers.
8. Biographical material in the Harwood papers.
9. Sadly these lecture notes have not survived.
10. Captain F.S. Bell, '*In Conclusion*', from *The Cruise of HMS Exeter*, produced as a decommissioning memoir at the end of the ship's last peacetime commission, for private circulation, by W.H. Smith of London; printed apparently in 1940. A copy is in the Harwood papers and provides a fascinating insight into British 'flag-showing' exercises on a distant station in the late 1930s.
11. Edelsten had first met Harwood in HMS *Southampton.* Letter to Millington-Drake in *Drama*, pp. 66–7.
12. Preface to Dudley Pope, *Battle of the River Plate* (Kimber, London, 1956).
13. !/40 undated, Harwood papers.
14 Harwood, para. 7.
15. For an account of this controversy, see Steven Roskill, *Naval Policy Between the Wars, Vol. 1: the Period of Anglo-American Antagonism 1919–29* (Collins, London, 1968).
16. For British cruiser details, see A. Raven and J. Roberts, *British Cruisers of World War Two* (Arms and Armour Press, London, 1980); for weaponry, Campbell, *Op Cit.*
17. Memo to Millington-Drake in the Millington-Drake Collection, I.W.M., Box 22. It is reproduced in *Drama*, pp. 263–6. It is not known how Lewin got his nickname 'Drunky'. He was a most distinguished naval airman, commanding two aircraft carriers before his last job as Director of Plans under Mountbatten as First Sea Lord. He retired in 1957 to take up a management post with Blackburns at Brough overseeing, among other projects, the Buccaneer programme.
18. *Ibid.*
19. 'Synopsis of signals', from a private collection of documents made available to the author by Robin Lumley via the British Maritime Charitable Foundation. The times for the battle are G.M.T. plus two hours, as used by the ships.
20. This does not appear in the Synopsis. Text from Pope, *Op. Cit.* the timing is from Harwood, para 10.

Chapter 5

1. The account of the action is based on the British battle summary with its detailed reports from Harwood and all three cruisers, and *The German Story*, together with the associated track charts. The British track chart was also printed in *The Battle of the River*

Plate: An Account of Events Before, During and After the Action, Up to the Destruction of the Admiral Graf Spee, effectively an expurgated version of the dispatches published by H.M.S.O., London in 1940. These have been supplemented by the material from both sides in *Drama* and an original German action report from *A Report of the Cruise of the Graf Spee*, apparently compiled in Buenos Aires under the auspices of the ship's senior officer and dated 25 May 1941. It was found by the U.S. Navy in December 1945 and is in P.R.O., ADM116/19292.

As is to be expected, there are major discrepancies between the various accounts, not least between the two track charts which are reproduced here. The British chart gives a good impression of what the British ships were doing and what they thought *Graf Spee* was doing, seen through their optical instruments over ranges of several miles; and the Germans, *vice versa* – with the added complication that the German chart seems to have been done largely from memory, as the senior navigation officer had destroyed 'vital papers' (the co-ordination sheet, action control notes, gunnery and torpedo control records) in Montevideo. The Author makes no claims to have produced a definitive account but he can reassure readers, it is based on a very thorough analysis and detailed consideration of the conflicting evidence.

2. There is correspondence with Woodhouse about *Graf Spee*'s 'critical speed' in Box 22 of the Millington-Drake Collection at the I.W.M.. Contemporary British intelligence reported a Petty Officer from the fore turret overheard in Buenos Aires as saying that vibration had been 'very bad' going into action and that the guns had been 'difficult to handle' while the ship was at full speed. ADM116/4320.
3. A hand-written memoir by M.C. Hill, kindly made available by Graham Beeson.
4. Harwood, para. 19.
5. Written to a friend 20 January 1940, quoted *Drama*, p. 191.
6. Report in P.R.O., ADM1/19192.
7. Like the other signals this is from the Synopsis in the Lumley Collection.
8. Harwood, para. 34.
9. See ADM1/19292. The most careful examination of the wreck by British specialists Kilroy and Purvis (see Chapter 12) seemed clearly to show the partial explosion of the shell and the severing of the cables; but the German report in the same file says the shell passed through without exploding and severed only the cable to the searchlight. On balance, the evidence seems to show a partial explosion and some cable damage. It is possible that the latter was increased as part of the scuttling process. On the other hand, Langmann, the German

Minister in Montevideo, while publicly underrating the damage to the ship, privately spoke of *Graf Spee* suffering serious fire control derangement. In truth, the loss of the main optical instrument was probably serious enough to qualify for this statement. The other cable damage caused by the 8-in. shell through the belt was repaired by 14 December, the day after the battle.

10. Translation from *Panzershiff Admiral Graf Spee* in Millington-Drake Collection, Box 24.
11. Dove, *Op. Cit.*
12. The diagrams attached to *The German Story* and the German Report in ADM1/19292 list hits in detail.
13. There is a diagrammatic lantern-slide in the Parry papers in the I.W.M. of these hits on the belt. Close British visual observation in Montevideo provided evidence for up to 50 British hits of various kinds on *Graf Spee*. Much work was done to see how far these corresponded with those found in the later British examination of the wreck, see ADM1/19292. This account, like others, is fundamentally based on the German hit diagram enclosed in *The German Story*, but it seems certain that more 6-in. hits, even if not damaging ones, were scored than those recorded there.

Chapter 6

1. The main sources for this section are as for the previous chapter.
2. Quoted in Pope, *Op. Cit.*
3. In letter of 20 January 1940, quoted in Millington-Drake, *Drama*, pp. 224–5.
4. M.C. Hill memoir.
5. The words quoted are from an interview Langsdorff granted to Cdr Eduardo Aumann of the Argentine Navy on the last day of his life. An English transcript is in the Millington-Drake Collection, Box 24.
6. Dove, *Op. Cit.*
7. Washbourne, *ibid.*
8. The matter is exhaustively covered by Millington-Drake in *Drama*, pp. 239–48. He concluded *Graf Spee* fired first, but the Author was impressed by the contrary testimony of both the commanding officer of the *Uruguay* and those in the French liner *Formose* who supported the German claim that *Achilles* fired first on this occasion. One can see some economical ambiguity in Washbourne's own account in his letter of 20 January, quoted in *Drama*, p. 240: 'It was bitter temptation. We were just outside the three-mile limit, that we admit, but inside the territorial waters claimed. Shortly after sunset, at 22,000 yards, *she gave us the excuse* (my italics) and with delight, I again muttered SHOOT! into my transmitter'.
9. Appendix No. 11 to *Achilles*'s report in the battle summary, para. 45.
10. Dove, Op. Cit.

Chapter 7

1. Whose collection, *Drama*, provides a major source for this chapter.

2. As described in a talk dated 13 December 1950, a script of which is in Box 24 of his papers at the I.W.M.
3. Admiral McCall wrote an account, '*The Trap*', for the part-work *Purnell's History of the Second World War*, pp. 57–62, that was also a useful source for this chapter.
4. Times are now Uruguayan Summer Time – G.M.T. plus three hours.
5. Telegram from Foreign Office to Millington-Drake, 1500 hrs, 15 December, copy in A.D.M. 116/4420.
6. The details of the radio organisation are covered in correspondence with Garland in Box 24 of the Millington-Drake papers in the I.W.M.
7. *Ibid.*
8. Report quoted in *Drama*, pp. 296–7.
9. *The German Story*, p. 18.
10. These are the figures in the report in ADM1/19292.
11. Rasenack in *Drama*, p. 457.
12. *Ibid.*
13. *Ibid.*
14. Harwood, para. 57. The signal was timed at 1135 hrs (Z plus 2).
15. McCall, '*Events Subsequent to the Action*', ADM223/69, and '*The Trap*', see Note 3, above.
16. Harwood, para. 65. The signal was timed 1615 hrs (Z plus 2).
17. McCall, '*The Trap*', p. 61.
18. Note 112 of 16 December, copy in Millington-Drake papers, Box 24.
19. Proposed annex to M. Blondel's book, *Entente Cordiale*. Millington-Drake papers, Box 24.
20. Telegram 165, 0502 hrs, 17 December 1939, ADM116/4470.
21. *Ibid.*
22. *Ibid.*
23. Telegram 92, 1630 hrs, 17 December 1939, ADM116/4470.
24. Letter to Foreign Office Librarian, Millington-Drake papers, ADM116/4470.

Chapter 8

1. From C.D. Bekker, *Swastika at Sea: The Struggle and Destruction of the German Navy 1939–45*, quoted in Drama, pp. 321–2.
2. *Führer Conferences on Naval Affairs 1939*, p. 60.
3. *Ibid.*, p. 61.
4. *The German Story*, p. 19.
5. Memorandum to Millington-Drake in *Drama*, p. 314.
6. *The German Story*, p. 20. See also *Drama*, pp. 330–31.
7. *Drama*, p. 331.
8. *The German Story*, pp. 21–3.
9. *Drama*, p. 331.
10. Rasenack, *Panzerschiff Graf Spee*, quoted in *Drama*, p. 334.
11. This important document is in the Millington-Drake papers at the I.W.M., Box 24.
12. From A. Campos, *Un Episodio de la Segundo Guerra Mondial*, quoted Drama, p. 336.
13. Harwood, para 71; signal received at 1540 hrs (Z plus 2).
14. Rasenack, *Op. Cit.*, quoted Drama, p. 338.
15. Term from interview, see Note 11.

16. Millington-Drake talk, 13 December 1950. Millington-Drake papers, Box 24.
17. '*Drama of the Graf Spee: Checkmate at Montevideo*', lecture handout, *ibid.*
18. Diary published in *Marinezeitung Leinen Los*, April 1960, and reprinted in *Drama*, pp. 347–8.
19. Letter to Millington-Drake quoted in *Drama*, p. 345.
20. Letter, 17 December 1939, Harwood papers.
21. Letter, 21 December 1939, Harwood papers.
22. Rasenack *Op. Cit.*, quoted in *Drama*, p. 346.
23. Millington-Drake talk, 13 December 1950, Millington-Drake papers, Box 24.
24. See Note 21.
25. Letter to Millington-Drake quoted *Drama*, p. 355.
26. Letter to a friend 20 January 1940, quoted *Drama*, p. 354.
27. Letter from Cdr H.D. Johnston to Millington-Drake, quoted *Drama*, p. 353.
28. Report of Lt Sghirla of *Zapican*, quoted *Drama* pp. 356–7.
29. Footnote, *Drama*, p. 356.
30. Letter, 21 December 1939. Harwood papers.
31. See Note 26.

Chapter 9

1. Rasenack *Panzerschiff Graf Spee* and Gotz's Diary quoted *Drama*, p. 363.
2. Rasenack, *Ibid.*
3. Note of 18 December 1939 recorded in Dispatch from Ambassador to the Foreign Office, London, Millington-Drake Papers, Box 24.
4. Gotz Diary, quoted *Drama*, p. 367.
5. Quoted Pope, *Battle of the River Plate*, p. 200.
6. Rasenack, *Op.Cit.*, quoted *Drama*, p. 367.
7. *The German Story*, pp. 25–6.
8. Details from 'Extract of a private letter to D.N.I. from N.A. Buenos Aires', ADM/223/69. It was from McCall quoting a 'report which I have received of a visit which a friend of mine paid to the Prefectura Maritima on the 20th of December for the purpose of obtaining information from the crew of the *Graf Spee* now interned in Buenos Aires'.
9. Dietrich, letter to Millington-Drake dated 26 January 1962 quoted in *Drama*, p. 369. He reported he found Langsdorff 'in full uniform stretched out on the flag of the Graf Spee'. McCall's 'friend' just reported 'a German flag'. See also Dr Harting's report below. McCall reported the Argentine Minister of Foreign Affairs telling the British Ambassador that Langsdorff had shot himself on 'the old Imperial German Flag' as hearsay in his later report NID0301/40 in ADM 116/4320. It seems inherently most unlikely that Langsdorff should have been carrying such a flag on active service; his last letter also makes clear his continuing loyalty to his Führer (to whom he

had taken a personal oath of allegiance) and that it was the contemporary German Naval ensign to whose honour he was referring.

10. Letter from Dr Harting to Millington-Drake, *Drama*, p. 464.

Chapter 10

1. Letter to DNI 22 December 1939, P.R.O., ADM223/69.
2. For the personal histories of internees, see *Drama*, pp. 375–90.

Chapter 11

1. ADM116/4320.
2. *Ibid.*
3. Quoted *Drama*, p. 393.
4. Letter to father of 11 January 1940, in Parry papers, I.W.M..
5. Details of homecomings from *Drama*, pp. 391–8.
6. Text in *Drama*, pp. 394–5.
7. Filmed newsreel of speech.
8. Correspondence in Millington-Drake papers, Box 22.

Chapter 12

1. Howse, *Radar at Sea, Op. Cit.*. The story of the purchase and examination of *Graf Spee* can be followed in ADM1/1922, ADM116/4472 and ADM116/5475, in the Public Records Office, London.
2. ADM116/5475.
3. *Ibid.*
4. Unattributed newspaper article, '*50-ton Gun is Raised from the Grave*', provided to the Author by Graham Beeson.

Chapter 13

1. Copy in Parry papers, I.W.M..
2. Memo quoted in *Drama*, p. 262.
3. Appendix V, *Drama*, pp. 457–8.
4. *Ibid.*, pp. 455–6.
5. Dispatch to the Foreign Office, 1 January 1940, Millington-Drake papers, Box 24.
6. *The German Story*, p. 15.
7. Appendix 1, *Drama*, pp. 441–4.
8. Telegram 182, 20 December 1939. Millington-Drake to U.K. Foreign Office, ADM116/4470.
9. Dispatch from Ambassador, 1 January 1940 in Millington-Drake papers, Box 24.
10. Quoted in letter 2/40/2a to Joan Harwood, Harwood papers.
11. *Ibid.*
12. Captain Fawcett Wray, considered one of the most brilliant officers of his time, had persuaded Admiral Troubridge not to engage *Goeben* as 'to risk glorious self-immolation would have put pride before his country's welfare'! See: G. Miller, *Superior Force* (Hull University Press 1996, p. 109).

Index